PATHWAYS
OF SPIRITUAL LIVING

Pathways
of Spiritual Living

SUSAN ANNETTE MUTO

IMAGE BOOKS
A Division of
Doubleday & Company, Inc.
Garden City, New York
1984

Library of Congress Cataloging in Publication Data
Muto, Susan Annette.
Pathways of spiritual living.
Bibliography: p. 187
1. Spiritual life—Catholic authors.   I. Title.
BX2350.2.M883   1984   248.4′82   84-1564
ISBN 0–385–19473–0

In memory of my father,

Frank Muto
(1904–1982)

May the Peace of the Lord
Be with him
Always

CONTENTS

ACKNOWLEDGMENTS

A book like this flows from the depths of one's own life always in dialogue with trusted colleagues and friends. Thus I acknowledge my gratitude to the faculty and staff of the Institute of Formative Spirituality at Duquesne University in Pittsburgh. Special thanks must be offered to Father Adrian van Kaam, C.S.Sp., Ph.D., Director Emeritus of the Institute, and Research Professor, for his help in readying the text for final publication. For their outstanding editorial contributions, I thank cordially Father Richard Byrne, O.C.S.O., Ph.D., a fellow faculty member, and Father Jim Carellas, pastor of Christ the Savior Orthodox Church, whose sensitive corrections and welcome suggestions I have incorporated into these pages. For her ongoing support and encouragement, heartfelt gratitude goes to Patricia Kossmann, Senior Editor, Doubleday & Company. Last but not least, I must express thanks to the faithful laity closest to me in life, the members of the Epiphany Association in Pittsburgh. To my mother, Helen Muto, I utter profound thanks. I am so grateful to her and to the unnamed but cherished friends who show me in a living way what it means to seek and serve the Lord.

PROLOGUE

> . . . all Christians in any state or walk of life are called to the
> fullness of Christian life and to the perfection of love, and by
> this holiness a more human manner of life is fostered also in
> earthly society.[1]

In the twenty years that have passed since the opening of the
Second Vatican Council, many changes have taken place in the
Church. Average Churchgoers may not know in detail how or
why these came about because they involve lengthy theological
investigation and study, the results of which only slowly filter
down to the faithful. One notices undoubtedly the obvious
changes in the liturgy and the celebration of the sacraments.
What keeps us on course in the upheaval of necessary renewal
are the underlying directives of our faith tradition, so richly
articulated in the documents of Vatican Council II.

No book could exhaust the wealth of insight contained in

1. Austin Flannery, O.P., general ed. Dogmatic Constitution on the Church *(Lumen
Gentium,* November 21, 1964), in *Vatican Council II: The Conciliar and Post
Conciliar Documents* (Collegeville, Minn.: Liturgical Press, 1975), p. 397. All
other Council documents will be quoted from this edition. Texts referring to
"laymen" or to "man" mean, of course, all laity, all persons.

these documents. One can only select a theme and develop it in further detail as I hope to do in this reflection on spiritual formation for Christians in the world. While drawing on the Vatican documents both for my definition of terms and for their inspirational content, I shall be relying primarily on the work I have done at the Institute of Formative Spirituality for the twenty years paralleling the Council's implementation of these decrees. At this center we enjoy the mingling in our graduate program of laity, religious, and clergy of many denominations and nations, who desire to deepen their own spiritual life and to develop skills in guiding others on their formation journey through teaching, spiritual direction, speaking, and writing.

Turning to *Lumen Gentium,* the Dogmatic Constitution on the Church, we find the following definition:

> The term "laity" is here understood to mean all the faithful except those in Holy Orders and those who belong to a religious state approved by the Church. That is, the faithful who by Baptism are incorporated into Christ, are placed in the People of God, and in their own way share the priestly, prophetic and kingly office of Christ, and to the best of their ability carry on the mission of the whole Christian people in the Church and in the world.[2]

While the document stresses the secular character proper to lay life, it insists on the close relation among laity, those ordained to the ministry of the priesthood, and members of religious congregations. Though celebrating this diversity of gifts, the document does state:

> . . . by reason of their special vocation it belongs to the laity to seek the kingdom of God by engaging in temporal affairs and directing them according to God's will. They live in the world, that is, they are engaged in each and every work and business of

2. Ibid., p. 388.

the earth and in the ordinary circumstances of social and family life which, as it were, constitute their very existence. There they are called by God that, being led by the spirit of the Gospel, they may contribute to the sanctification of the world, as from within like leaven, by fulfilling their own particular duties. Thus, especially by the witness of their life, resplendent in faith, hope and charity they must manifest Christ to others. It pertains to them in a special way so to illuminate and order all temporal things with which they are so closely associated that these may be effected and grow according to Christ and may be to the glory of the Creator and Redeemer.[3]

What interests me most in these and related texts is the stress placed on the laity's appraisal of *"the inner nature, the value and the ordering of the whole of creation to the praise of God."*[4] I sense in this emphasis a call to integrate my professional activity with my yearning for a deeper spiritual life. Daily functioning ought to aid greater holiness. Being filled with the spirit of Christ ought to enable us to effect justice, peace, and mercy in the world. The document states in no uncertain terms:

> The laity enjoy a principle role in the universal fulfillment of this task. Therefore, by their competence in secular disciplines and by their activity, interiorly raised up by grace, let them work earnestly in order that created goods through human labor, technical skill and civil culture may serve the utility of all men according to the plan of the creator and the light of his word. May these goods be more suitably distributed among all men and in their own way may they be conducive to universal progress in human and Christian liberty. Thus, through the members of the Church, will Christ increasingly illuminate the whole of human society with his saving light.[5]

3. Ibid., p. 389.
4. Ibid., p. 393 (italics mine).
5. Ibid., p. 393.

The texts I have quoted will serve as the primary inspiration for this book. I propose to focus on the call to holiness because I believe it may be neglected in our eagerness to engage in human activity. The pressures of life may lead us to forget that we are called to "witness before the world to the resurrection and life of the Lord Jesus."[6] Each of us is to be a sign of the living God. Together, yet uniquely, each one to the best of his or her ability must nourish the world with spiritual fruits, or, as the document says in summary, quoting St. John Chrysostom, "In a word: 'what the soul is in the body, let Christians be in the world.' "[7]

It is necessary, I feel, to retrace some of the stages and conditions that can help us as laity to hear the universal call to holiness and to maintain a fervent spiritual life in the midst of secular pursuits. In this book we will trace some foundations of spiritual formation that enable us to model our life on Christ's example of holiness and to serve his kingdom more joyfully and effectively. These foundations include, among others, silence, solitude, prayer, liturgical celebration, spiritual reading, meditation, contemplation, participation, and social presence. I will draw upon insights that have emerged in my teaching experience with clergy, laity, and religious over the years as well as upon the published and unpublished texts and lectures of my Institute colleagues, most notably Father Adrian van Kaam.

Because a book, to be real, must arise in some way from the biography of its author, I will try to share with my readers my own struggles as a laywoman to integrate spiritual life and service. Here I am mindful of another document, the Decree on the Apostolate of Lay People.[8] In the section on spirituality it says:

6. Ibid., p. 395.
7. Ibid., p. 396.
8. *Apostolicam Actuositatem,* 18 November 1965, in Flannery, op. cit., pp. 766–98.

This life of intimate union with Christ in the Church is maintained by the spiritual helps common to all the faithful, chiefly by active participation in the liturgy. Laymen should make such a use of these helps that, while meeting their human obligations in the ordinary conditions of life, they do not separate their union with Christ from their ordinary life; but through the very performance of their tasks, which are God's will for them, actually promote the growth of their union with him. This is the path along which laymen must advance, fervently, joyfully, overcoming difficulties with prudent patient efforts. Family cares should not be foreign to their spirituality, nor any other temporal interest; in the words of the apostle: "Whatever you are doing, whether speaking or acting, do everything in the name of the Lord, Jesus Christ, giving thanks to God the Father through him." (Col. 3:17)[9]

Such a life demands nothing less than the continuous exercise of faith, hope, and charity; it calls for meditation on the word of God and on the cross and resurrection of the Lord; it invites us to express concretely in our lives the spirit of the Beatitudes, to imitate the hidden, humble Christ and the apostolic spiritual life of his Holy Mother, Mary. Only in this way can we "exert all [our] energies in extending God's kingdom, in making the Christian spirit a vital energizing force in the temporal sphere."[10] With this goal of harmonious living before us, let us begin our formation journey.

---

9. Ibid., p. 770.
10. Ibid. The Beatitudes, along with the evangelical counsels pertaining to obedience (listening to the will of the Father); poverty (wisely using things as gifts of God while acknowledging our dependency on him); and chastity (loving others with an attitude of reverence and responsibility according to one's committed lifestyle), are and remain salient guidelines for lay spirituality. I've concentrated on the Beatitudes as "attitudes of being" in my book *Blessings That Make Us Be: A Formative Approach to Living the Beatitudes* (New York: Crossroad Publishing Co., 1982).

PATHWAYS
OF SPIRITUAL LIVING

1

Beginnings

And his teaching made a deep impression on them because, unlike the scribes, he taught them with authority. (Mk. 1:22)[1]

1. Alexander Jones, general ed. *The Jerusalem Bible* (Reader's Edition) (Garden City, N.Y.: Doubleday & Co., Inc., 1966). All biblical references in my book are taken from this edition.

"A deep impression . . ." Why do these words evoke an immediate response in me? Is it because relatively few things impress me that much? Days fade into weeks, weeks into months, and I remember so little of what happens to me. While most moments come and go, some do leave a deep impression. I recall my nephew's hand clasped in mine in total trust as we entered a crowded arena to see the circus. I return in memory to a solitary walk by the sea that changed my sorrow to anticipation; to dinner with a friend seldom seen but always present in my heart; to the words of a sincere, self-giving teacher, who, like Jesus, spoke with authority. This person truly became an author of my life. Something he said compelled me to make a fresh start, a new beginning in my thinking.

A good film can have a similar effect. Through the right

blending of sound and silence, character development, crisis and resolution, the director helps the audience to break through illusions about life as one thinks it ought to be to an encounter with the way it really is. Joy, we learn, is not a steady, euphoric state, but a moment of splendor that makes a deep impression on us.

What are these moments like in relation to the spiritual life? Some are shared; others are silent. Though I love being with others, I find myself drawn to pray in silence, to become more recollected before the Lord. In a world fast changing, in a society characterized by mobility and uprootedness, I yearn to rest in God, to hear anew what Jesus taught, to live these lessons more fully in daily life.

For laypersons the call to holiness, issued by Vatican Council II, is more than a pious directive to a few gifted Christians. This call has universal implications pertaining to a spirituality for the laity *as* laity. In the history of the Church, one can witness the establishment of religious life in desert hermitages and in communities, followed by the emergence of special schools of spirituality evolved by great founders like St. Francis or St. Ignatius. A variety of communal, clerical, monastic, and apostolic styles of living are open to laity desirous of becoming priests, brothers, or sisters.

Rich as these models are, profound as their contribution to the history of spiritual formation is, they are able to offer only limited guidelines for a distinctively *lay* spirituality lived for the kingdom in the midst of the world. Too often lay people are inclined to equate spirituality with a monastic model as such or with an apostolic stress on doing extra things, like making a retreat or immersing oneself in special programs or righteous causes. They have difficulty integrating their spiritual desires with their routine duties.

I've asked myself again and again if there really is anything holy about doing the dishes, or planning a party, or preparing a class. These paltry secular projects seem far removed from the ecstasy of contemplative union. Common sense usually prevails over false guilt in this regard, for I realize that no one lives on the mountaintop all the time. Most of life occurs in the ditches and trenches of pedestrian routine. It is here that we must respond to the Lord's call if we are to find the real meaning of an everyday spirituality lived in the world and not inflict upon ourselves an unrealistic model based on someone else's gifts. Single people as well as married couples are struggling to hear God's word and to obey his voice in keeping with their own gifts and with Christ's invitation to share in his priestly, prophetical, and kingly office.

Our life in the world means loving God *as* and *where* we are. Jesus did not address himself to a spiritual elite but to all who heard his voice and allowed his words to touch and change their hearts. His teaching is full of hope for average people because he always promised them they could begin again despite their failure. There was no end to God's merciful forgiveness.

We need to reclaim the basics of a Christian spirituality that are at once timely and timeless. These directives can be incarnated by housekeepers and professors, truck drivers and technicians, salespersons and poets, whenever and wherever they live. All can pray; all can proclaim the kingdom while carrying on their work in the world. The key to this integration involves awakening to the presence of the transcendent *in* the actual here and now situation. It is as if we live simultaneously in two orders of reality: the invisible *and* the visible, the infinite *and* the finite, the eternal *and* the temporal. We come to know the world in which we live as the house of God. We try to combine solitude and communion, silence and spiritual reading, absorption in God and response to his will.[2]

---

2. For an application of these directives to the life of single persons in the world, see my book *Celebrating the Single Life: A Spirituality for Single Persons in Today's World* (Garden City, N.Y.: Doubleday & Co., Inc., 1982).

It is the mission of Christians to preserve these basic spiritual values and to pass them on from generation to generation. Living Christlike dispositions in an ordinary, steady, faithful way is not always exciting. Jesus' words make a deep impression on us because what he teaches is perennial, lasting, basic truth. He points out in lively stories and examples that pride has to give way to humility, that we must move from possessiveness to liberation, from stingy selfishness to self-giving love.

In this regard I recall reading a brief text by St. John of the Cross that has echoed in my mind for many years. It is from his *Sayings of Light and Love:* "Well and good if all things change, Lord God, provided we are rooted in You."[3] Like many children of my generation, I've lived through profound changes in consciousness capsulized in what we term the space age. Growing up, my brothers and I were awed by the test patterns and faded figures flashed on the television screen. In a few short years we've come to take for granted technology sophisticated enough to launch the space shuttle. Fantasies evoked by science fiction have long since become reality. No wonder we feel confused by the speed of change. Nothing is as we knew it, whether one refers to liturgical ceremonies or sexual mores, to advanced technology or styles of family living.

Discoveries by the differential sciences in physics, medicine, and psychology mark progress, humanly speaking. Yet experience tells us that this same progress may lead to spiritual regression. It is easy to forget the mystery behind the ongoing formation of universe and world when one feels swept along by tides of change, incapable of slowing down the speed-driven pace. As fear of the unknown builds, we need to be wary of any conservative backlash, for many, if not most, of these

---

3. *The Collected Works of St. John of the Cross,* trans. Kieran Kavanaugh, O.C.D., and Otilio Rodriguez, O.C.D. (Washington, D.C.: Institute of Carmelite Studies, ICS Publications, 1973), p. 669. Hereafter referred to as *Collected Works of St. John.*

changes are for the good. The vision of Planet Earth makes us more responsive to world hunger. Thanks to breakthrough medical research, infants born today will live healthier, longer lives than at any time in the past. We are more mindful than ever of the global desire for world peace and why each of us in his or her own way must contribute to this effort. These are only a few examples that validate the first part of St. John's saying: "Well and good if all things change, Lord God . . ." But his saying does not stop there, nor can we.

The provision suggests that this changing life is good on the condition that we root ourselves in the changeless love, guidance, and mercy of God. Nothing remains static in the temporality of human existence, but we are not only creatures of time; we are bound to and for eternity. Thus no matter how many things change, we must not forget our dependency on God. He alone can satisfy our desire for consonance and harmony with all that is.

Recalling my past, focusing on the present, anticipating the future, I can honestly say that nothing stays the same. I may notice change in small or large ways. Personally I may be more patient with myself and others. Socially I may let go of my illusions of what should be and take more time to listen to what is, responding flexibly to each situation. Instead of resisting change, I befriend it. Who of us can predict what the Lord may ask when we abandon ourselves heart and soul to him?

Such abandonment enables us to place life's changes in their proper perspective. As one friend reminded me, "There is a meaning to this mess, even if we don't always see it." Peace and courage are possible if I keep the Lord as my true foundation. If I return to him in silence, reading, meditation, prayer, and contemplation, I will not lose my moorings in the fast flow. Endings will become beginnings. So what if all things change, myself included, provided I am rooted in him?

Whether standing still or moving forward, I can try to incarnate divine directives in my active style of life, marked as it is by a graceful rhythm of stillness and service. Then active participation will become simultaneously a way of practicing the presence of God.[4]

This sense of being rooted in the Holy is basic to spiritual formation. Though our lives take a variety of turns, we all share the same starting point, articulated so beautifully in the Book of Genesis:

> God created man in the image of himself, in the image of God he created him, male and female he created them. (Gn. 1:27)

We are all made in the image or form of God. His benevolence enables us to return to him, no matter how many times we turn away. He draws us from the depths of betrayal to the heights of union, provided we root ourselves more and more in the Word made Flesh, the fullest image of the Father, the bridge between us and God. Our attitude must be that of the Christ whose

> . . . state was divine, yet he did not cling to his equality with God but emptied himself to assume the condition of a slave, and became as men are . . . (Ph. 2:6–7)

God made us in his likeness, though we in our freedom may draw away from him in gestures of disobedience and prideful self-sufficiency. Through the passion, death, and resurrection of Jesus, the likeness between us is restored. Though salvation is ours, though forgiveness is ours, the reality of our fallen condition means that the quest for holiness lasts a lifetime.

Fortunately grace facilitates this quest as we follow the paths of spiritual deepening that have helped people over the ages to regain the union of likeness lost by sin. These condi-

4. The actual "how to" of fostering this presence is articulated more fully in a book coauthored with Adrian van Kaam entitled *Practicing the Prayer of Presence* (Denville, N.J.: Dimension Books, 1980).

tions are as basic for laypersons as for priests and religious. Our union with God is not in question. It is substantiated by the sheer fact of our creation. We *are* because of his love. What is marred by sin is the union of likeness, as the words of St. John of the Cross explain.

> . . . In discussing union with God, we are not discussing the substantial union which is always existing, but the union and transformation of the soul in God. This union is not always existing, but we find it only where there is likeness of love. We will call it "the union of likeness," and the former "the essential or substantial union."[5]

As this text implies, the goal of the spiritual life is to restore with God's help the likeness of love. The first and foremost avenue to this restoration is following Christ, whose life we are called as Christians to emulate. St. Paul wrote of this imitation in his epistle to the Ephesians.

> Try, then, to imitate God, as children of his that he loves, and follow Christ by loving as he loved you, giving himself up in our place *as a fragrant offering and a sacrifice to God.* (Ep. 5:1–3)[6]

The aspects of Jesus' life that are particularly appealing to me as a Christian in the world are his hiddenness, his sense of detachment, and his surrender to the Father. Though you and I may be known in our circle of family and friends, we live for the most part a spirituality that participates in the hidden life of Jesus of Nazareth. He chose to witness to this ordinary way for the first thirty years of his life, only then entering into public ministry. In the hiddenness of family life, he blessed the

5. *Collected Works of St. John,* book 2, *The Ascent of Mount Carmel,* chapt. 5, p. 116.
6. See also Thomas à Kempis, *The Imitation of Christ,* ed. Harold C. Gardiner (Garden City, N.Y.: Doubleday & Co., Inc., Image Books, 1955). This much-loved favorite of laypersons, some say second only to the Bible, still offers us insights of perennial worth pertaining to the way of imitation. I've analyzed this way in my book *Steps Along the Way: The Path of Spiritual Reading* (Denville, N.J.: Dimension Books, 1975).

daily existence in and through which we too find our sanctification.

From the beginning of his public life, starting with his days in the desert, Jesus manifested a sense of detachment from worldly powers and possessions. Through renunciation he gained true liberation, establishing for his followers the art of being fully in the world while not being of the world. Paradoxical as it may seem, powerlessness becomes a source of true power. Poverty of spirit makes us rich in reflection and prayer. Resistance to secular wealth and fame enabled him and us, his followers, to respond to God's offer of lasting treasure.

Jesus' surrender became a source of strength. He was not afraid to stand up for his beliefs, even at the risk of his life. His courage inspires us when we find ourselves in a position to compromise our commitments. Christian mothers and fathers, professionals in medicine, law, industry, and academics must struggle as I do to maintain and live a committed Christianity *in* the world without giving way to the will *of* the world. Like Jesus we want to listen to what the Father asks of us, knowing all the while that this may mean the suffering of loneliness, misunderstanding, betrayed promises, and dashed pride.

Hiddenness, detachment, surrender—these are three foundations of Christian formation that facilitate a spirituality lived joyfully and effectively in the world while not becoming merely worldly. Other avenues to Christian living, modeled by Jesus for our sakes, include taking time to be present to God in silence, meditation, prayer, and contemplation. These moments of listening ready us to respond to others in charity and compassion. In this way we journey homeward to the Father, leaving behind us slowly and gradually the land of unlikeness and turning toward the land of likeness.[7]

7. For a further treatment of this frequently used metaphor, made most popular by the Cistercian Fathers, see Aelred Squire, *Asking the Fathers: The Art of Meditation and Prayer* (New York: Paulist Press, 1973). I've also dealt with the journey

The call to holiness beckons us to return to the basics, that is, to those conditions for fostering single-hearted, awe-filled, grateful abandonment to God's will, revealed in the midst of our life in the everyday world. Whatever our obligations, professionally or socially speaking, whatever our degree of success or failure, wealth or poverty, fame or hiddenness, we come from God and we are returning to him. This is the inescapable foundation of our journey from birth to death.

Of course the urgency of time overtakes us. Of course we forget the eternal. Of course old habits are hard to reform. We can think of a thousand excuses not to pursue a spiritual life, but the price we pay for such escapism is high. It is better to take a few steps forward, even if we fall several behind; it is better to try and fail than never to try at all. None of us is or ever will be perfect. That is why we need God.

However pressured we feel by change, however many complaints we voice about the harshness of life and the crowded condition of our schedules, there is no excuse in the long run to remain an hour-a-Sunday Christian. We are called to so much more. God is not the Wholly Other from whom we must hide. He is the most intimate center of our lives. We can resist him and refuse to listen, or we can surrender, freed from the burden of self-sufficiency, to his waiting embrace. The choice is ours, and somewhere, at some time, every one of us must make it.

Characteristic of Christian living in the world is a rhythm or flow from inspiration to incarnation, from prayer to participation, from contemplation to action.[8] Consonance is at least glimpsed when time becomes our servant rather than our being enslaved to time; when possessions no longer possess us;

---

theme in my book *The Journey Homeward: On the Road of Spiritual Reading* (Denville, N.J.: Dimension Books, 1977).

8. These rhythms are the focus of my book *Renewed at Each Awakening: The Formative Power of Sacred Words* (Denville, N.J.: Dimension Books, 1979).

when gratification occurs in and through responsible relationships. Such consonance in our Christian formation is only possible when we root ourselves more deeply in the foundations of our faith tradition.[9] Functional effectiveness flows from spiritual affection. Prayer energizes us for professional activity.

This integration of mind and heart, of intuition and talent, is the unvoiced goal we seek, especially in our professions. Any split between spirituality and labor will harm us in the long run. The life goes out of what we do, and we wonder why nothing matters that much to us any more. Paradoxically, this point of ego despair is the beginning of a felt desire for inner restoration. Too often we blame what is happening to us on outside forces beyond our control. We refuse to look within and face who we are, what we really hope to become. Naively we seek a magic formula for renewal that will resolve all tensions. Neither pursuing spectacular solutions to inner disillusion nor stagnating in worn-out customs and routines will solve the dilemma. There must be more to life than merely going through the motions.

Maybe the way out means going more deeply into the resources that comprise our Christian heritage: the treasures of wisdom embedded in the scriptures, in the writings of the spiritual masters, in the liturgical and sacramental life. In these sources we will find ourselves in the deepest sense.

Charles de Foucauld wrote to his sister on October 13, 1899,

> if souls consecrated to God, monks who meditate on perfection from morning to night, feel the need, to the end of their lives, of reading and rereading the works of the great Masters of the spiritual life and the lives of the saints, their forerunners,

9. I am indebted here to Adrian van Kaam's distinction between faith and formation traditions. A faith tradition hands down from generation to generation foundational beliefs and values pertaining to the overall meaning of life and world. These admittedly remote directives are put into concrete practice in words and symbols that comprise a specific formation tradition.

how much more have those the need that have to live in the world in the midst of so many distracting preoccupations.[10]

While reading these texts, we try to remain open to directives in them pertaining to our current situation and our call to holiness. The two go hand in hand, accounting for the different amounts of time spent in spiritual reading by a monk, a married person, a single Christian. Each one in each situation has a different set of limits and possibilities. What matters is that we set as our goal to foster this practice and to temper the preoccupations that prevent it.

Often I don't feel like writing. What would make me feel good is going out for a walk. But if I did not sit at my desk and write for a while, nothing would be produced. It is not a question of either-or but of both-and. I sit and write and then go for a walk or vice versa. Is this incident not similar to what happens in the spiritual life? I perform so much better when I take time to read, reflect, meditate, and pray as preparation for my work. Without this flow of leisurely presence, leading to effective labor, my entire day is energy-draining. I tend to be more impatient than compassionate, more irritable than gentle, more functionalistic than attentively effective.

Our spiritual life cannot develop in isolation. De Foucauld's point is that we need to be in touch with others who have lived the life of the spirit too. We need to foster a living in-touchness with the text in some way. The alternative is to settle for a superficial life of sensual gratification, accumulation of material wealth, control, power, insincerity, repression. The list could go on, but it is clear to all of us what happens when we sever ourselves from the Sacred and therewith from our possibility to live a more humane, wholesome, concerned life. Anything less is antithetical to the Christian ideal in which the

10. Charles de Foucauld, *Meditations of a Hermit*, trans. Charlotte Balfour (New York: Orbis Books, 1981), p. 146.

dispositions of humility, honesty, and charity prevail. Such values last. They open us to what really matters in life.

On Pentecost, June 6, 1897, the Lord communicated to Charles de Foucauld what was to be the essence of his vocation. Imprinted on his heart by the voice of his Master were foundations of spiritual living we too can emulate:

> Love of God and forgetfulness of self in joyful contemplation of my glory; compassion and grief for my sufferings; joy in my joy; grief for sins committed against me, and a burning desire to see me glorified in every soul. Love of your brother for my sake who loves all men as a father loves his children. To wish for my sake for the spiritual and material good of all men. Freedom, liberty of speech, tranquillity, peace. All for God's sake, nothing for your own sake or any other creature's.[11]

These are the priorities of Christian living, as right for laity as for religious. For Charles the primary reality was the love relation between him and God. From that center flowed all other commitments. Around that core he planned how to spend his time, the hours of prayer, the hours of service. He was able, therefore, to experience directly the power of divine formation. When Charles was alone in the desert, Jesus became his director. He talked continually to the Lord, and the Lord graciously responded. At times Charles doubted himself, but the Master assured him that his vocation was to preach the Gospel in silence in imitation of the hidden life in Nazareth.

God could form Charles because he acknowledged his creatureliness, his abjection, his utter dependency. He did not resist aridity but accepted it as a time of waiting upon God's word. He gave up the human need to be in control and gave into the mystery of God's will. He lived on the borderline between the timeless and time and spent his lay life retracing

11. Ibid., p. 130.

Jesus' steps from Bethlehem, to Nazareth, to the Mount of Calvary, to the resurrected glory of Easter.

Charles experienced the transcendent, inexhaustible love of God that pours into creation. Just as he held himself in readiness to receive this love, its demands and delights, so must we. We too can open ourselves to the forming power of the word, to the transforming power of grace. This readiness is essential if we are to follow Jesus' journey from silence to service. Only if we are willing to go into the desert can we be witnesses to God in the world.[12]

The desert, as Charles discovered, is the place where God discloses his directives to our heart. The desert is not only a geographical place like the Sahara. It is a metaphor signifying an experience of dislocation and disclosure. God jars us out of our complacency and compels us to appraise our calling. He grants us the grace of ego desperation. We feel the floor dropping from us, the controls slipping away. Perhaps the cause is physical illness, a failure of some sort, a signal from within that we must change the course of our life. Perhaps we are experiencing burnout or mid-life crisis. Whatever the occasion, dislocation is the result. We are in the desert, feeling doubtful, discouraged, dry. In our desperation we can grow bitter or become more pliable to God's forming hand, as clay responds to the potter's touch.

Surrendering to the solitude readies us to receive new disclosures. God may assure us of his love, renew our faith, rekindle courage. He may tell us that the hidden life is a noble calling, that he appreciates our work, even if others are thankless. He collects the fragments of our life and puts them together in the wide-open space of the desert. In the light of his transcen-

---

12. For validation of this point in a classical and a contemporary text, see Thomas Merton, trans., *The Wisdom of the Desert: Sayings from the Desert Fathers of the Fourth Century* (London: Sheldon Press, 1974) and Carlo Carretto, *Letters from the Desert,* trans. Rose Mary Hancock (Maryknoll, N.Y.: Orbis Books, 1972).

dence, we are able to regain perspective. Thus the desert, which appears so dry, is actually the one place that refreshes.

I was more than ever convinced of this fact when I went to the Holy Land for the first time. The desert is hot and arid but hauntingly beautiful. It is not sterile but teeming with life. Under the talented care of a generation of dedicated workers, the desert blooms and becomes productive. For a Christian pilgrim like myself, Israel is a powerful symbol of the Paschal Mystery. The desert is paradox. Contraries coincide. Renunciation is liberation. Weakness is strength. Darkness is light. Stillness is dancing. Dying is rising. The stones in the desert are densely silent, yet they speak of the Lord's presence there.

I understood why Jesus wanted to go to these lonely places and pray for a while. In the silence of the night, he could listen in peace to the Father's word. He would not betray his calling by attending only to the clamor of the crowd. He was more than a physical healer or a future king. He was the One destined from the beginning to bridge the abyss between humanity and God caused by sin. The terror and beauty of that mission must have gripped him during those long, lonely desert nights. He needed to be there, to feel the Father's embrace. Strengthened by his love, so amply bestowed in this stark silence, he could return to the people and respond to their needs.

What I have described in this chapter, at least implicitly, is a foundational pattern of Christian formation—the stages of which I want to develop more fully in the remainder of this book. The pattern is at once circular and progressive. We move back and forth, down and around, while inching ahead. Our aim is to reclaim these foundations of formative spirituality in such a way that we really experience silence as an inner condition for listening to the word; listening as an invitation to reflection; reflection as an avenue to friendly discourse with

God; prayer as an opening for infused contemplation; and contemplation as the only reliable ground on which our activities can grow into service of the Lord. Let us continue this formation journey by going with Jesus into the desert.

2

Desert Messages

In the morning, long before dawn, he got up and left the house, and went off to a lonely place and prayed there. (Mk. 1:35)

Every summer I try to spend at least a few weeks at the shore. Nothing restores my equilibrium better than the ocean. As night inches toward the dawn, I too leave my room and go off alone to walk beside the sea. Thoughts ebb and flow with the rhythm of the waves. Soon I feel more quiet within. I pray not so much with words as with silent rejoicing and a sense of awe before the immense mystery and goodness of God. I experience a longing for nearness to him and a simple, steady desire to stay on the course he wants me to follow.

These touches of intimacy may last but a moment, but they are imprinted deeply on my memory. Now, as I cross the sand, lit by full sunshine, I feel as if I have been tuned in, however briefly, to what life is all about. After breakfast, in the midst of doing this or that, I pause and remember the morning, like one recalls the sweet, solemn refrain of a favorite symphony.

Merely the remembrance energizes me to go about my work. This is what I mean by a desert moment, and I suspect that something like it was experienced by Jesus.

The desert never ceased to attract him. One imagines him wandering around there as a boy, exploring ridges and caverns as boys are wont to do. A few years later, at the start of his public ministry, he would be tested by Satan for forty days in this wilderness, where, as scripture says, "He was with the wild beasts, and the angels looked after him" (Mk. 1:13). No doubt he withdrew to the desert frequently, not only to pray but also to escape the misunderstanding and worldly acclaim he evoked in crowds clamoring for more attention to their social or political problems.

How can we account for this attraction? Why is it so basic to our becoming prayerful, socially responsive Christians? If we return with Jesus to the beginning of his ministry, we may find the answers we are seeking.

The Judean countryside, Jerusalem, the Jordan River, Nazareth—these places are no longer sites specified on a map but living realities. While in the Holy Land, I traversed the countryside where Jesus grew to maturity: the fields and caves around Bethlehem; Tiberius and the Sea of Galilee; the narrow streets of the old city, the way of the cross. Everywhere I encountered reminders of Jesus' earthly life. I imagined him leaving Nazareth and journeying up to Jerusalem, where he would face his destiny. I experienced him more and more as fully human and fully divine.

One day I drove from Jerusalem to the Dead Sea. The weather was stifling. The wind blowing through the car window was hot and dry. I concentrated on the ribbonlike road, watching heat waves rise from its surface. The sand was beige, then red, then burnished gold, depending on how the light bounced from rock formation to flat land. Occasionally I would spot a patch of green where the wasteland bloomed, but mostly I was surrounded by hot, blowing sand.

The desert began to affect me. Thoughts about its meaning started to form. It became a powerful symbol, revealing many levels of meaning. Sorting these through, I found myself concentrating on two words: *desperation* and *delight*. These sum up my experience during that drive, and I think they have a lot to do with developing a lay spirituality.

When we follow Jesus into the desert, we are likely to experience what could be called ego desperation. Basically this means acknowledging that our life is not nor ever will be completely under our control. Even the thought of control is ludicrous in the desert. It is so much more immense and powerful than we are. We feel so small driving through it, so dependent on forces beyond our control. God forbid, I thought, if this car should break down. What would I do? A short time in this heat and dryness could be disastrous for a city dweller like myself.

In the desert the pillars of human power, pleasure, and possession are smashed. One feels powerless, miles away from sources of immediate gratification, the owner of little or nothing of material value. One cannot barter one's way out of loneliness and silence. One can only wait until it passes on the wings of faith and hope.

It no longer surprised me that Jesus was able to resist the demon's empty promises of earthly success. What good would fame be in the desert? Survival here is not a matter of illusory attachment to material supports but of focusing on the spiritual life, which is to say of living in the reality of our sheer dependency on a mystery much greater than we are. Jesus called this forming mystery the Father's will. His surrender to it made him strong enough to resist demonic temptation. In this way he moved from seeming desperation to delight. What appeared to be weakness was really strength. He could only conduct his ministry if he remained in union with the will of the Father.

To say that ego desperation is really a source of spiritual delight is another way of saying that if we cease to rely only on our own controlling egos and surrender to God, we will not be disappointed. He will form us into his servants. The desperation we feel in our personal desert moments should not give way to discouragement or despair. This experience teaches us that failures and imperfections are not insurmountable obstacles to God; paradoxically they are conditions for the possibility of enjoying true intimacy.

The drive to the Dead Sea was not only a symbol of human dependency on divine sustenance; it was also a delightful source of praise and adoration. At a certain point I pulled over to a lookout and beheld the desert in all its beauty. The flowing dunes, the sage-sweet smell, the towering hills gnarled by years of resistance to wind and erosion—all formed a mighty chorus proclaiming God's presence in creation. Freed from the illusion of worldly power, one is free to play before the face of the Father. How liberated Jesus must have felt when he left the desert after those forty days of prayer and fasting. With what zeal he must have approached his public ministry. The desert may dry up our pride, but only for the sake of preparing us for true discipleship and the spiritual delights it entails.

One of these is repentance. I mean more than occasional sorrow for this or that sin. I mean repenting that we are inclined to forget God in this fast-paced, functionalized world. The desert reminds us that we belong to him. It mocks any illusion that we can rely ultimately on ourselves. We are weak, wounded, finite, dying creatures. The desert in its stark reality awakens our sense of repentance.

The desert initiates us into the life of the spirit by helping us to discover who we most deeply are. To follow Christ means that we must let go of excessive attachments to passing pleasures and possessions, to ploys of autonomous power, to tangible goods as if they were ultimate. Christ asks us to abandon our idols, whatever they may be, and to love him with our entire being.

Like the first disciples, we have to abandon our nets and enter into the desert of detachment and surrender. We need to be released by his grace from whatever prevents us from following him. What the Lord offers us is an admittedly frightening program of ego stripping, but this wounding is a prescription for more personal wholeness.

In the desert the Lord asks us if we want to live the life of the spirit in the abstract, as if it were a collection of clear-cut rules, or if we want to live this life in the concrete, challenging, creative ambiguity of everyday life in the world. It is one thing to know the do's and don'ts pertaining to formation in Christ, but what if our knowledge does not carry over into our actions? We claim that we want God to direct us, we start off with good intentions, but what if we find ourselves persistently missing the mark?

We may veer from vague attraction to a perfectionistic model of spirituality toward the flabbiest sort of laxity, from too much discipline to none at all. This perverse tendency to heroism is but another form of pride. It tempts us to push against the pace of grace in our lives. The solution is not to cultivate the opposite extreme of laziness but to engage in modest asceticism in tune with the appeals and challenges of grace.

By living a balanced spirituality, we avoid one or the other extreme. We adore God's ineffable mystery while gratefully acknowledging his tender mercy. We move from calculations about how to be perfect to compassion for our own and others' wounded condition. Though laypersons as a rule cannot leave behind their professional and familial responsibilities and disappear into the desert, they can create hermitage moments amidst the noisy demands of everyday life.

For example, a married man can pray

Lord, give me the courage to follow you as the head of my family. Grant me the grace I need to break the bonds of exalted expectations. Teach me to cling to you so that I will not shirk my responsibility to care for those you've entrusted to me. When I fall because of weakness, be merciful to me, a sinner. Patiently pick me up. Help me to start anew, to live no longer by the gauge of worldly gain but to remember that your grace is the source of my humble accomplishment.

The desert is a living symbol for us of the integration of prayer and participation, of contemplation and action. When the burden of bearing Jesus' message becomes exhausting, we can do as he did and go off to a lonely place, at least by retiring to the desert of our heart, to refresh ourselves in prayer. In moments of physical, functional, or spiritual darkness, we can call out to the Father, echoing Jesus' words, "My God, my God, why have you deserted me?" (Mt. 27:47). Speaking of this moment, when Jesus felt utterly forsaken by the Father, St. John of the Cross said:

[It was] the most extreme abandonment, sensitively, that He had suffered in His life. And by it He accomplished the most marvelous work of His whole life . . . He brought about the reconciliation and union of the human race with God through grace.[1]

Though we may feel as deserted as Jesus did, we must retain the faith that our God has never been more near than he is now.

God knows that we cannot help ourselves in such desert moments. He knows that we need him to be with us. Whatever

1. *The Ascent of Mount Carmel,* book 2, chapt. 7, in *Collected Works of St. John,* p. 124.

it is that threatens to deplete us he can transform into a source of new hope and courage. His purpose, expressed so beautifully by Isaiah, is to "let the wilderness and the dry lands exult,/let the wasteland rejoice and bloom . . ." (Is. 35:1). Ego desperation is painful, but it does prevent us from remaining complacent. It is easy to take God for granted when we feel that we can control our destiny.

Illness or failure, any form of personal deprivation, reminds us of our need for him. These events are desert messengers, heralding the Transcendent. They tell us to pause a while, to turn to God in prayer, to reappraise our life direction. The courage to start again may be contingent upon our willingness to step aside and engage in self-appraisal. To know who we are and where we are going may require that we literally go off to a solitary place for reflection and prayer. Strengthened by this contact with God, we may regain our sense of purpose.

I believe that our being in the desert evokes the mercy of God. In the desert he cannot help but respond to our misery. By the same token, we can be more compassionate to ourselves and to others who are in the same relatively lost situation. In stillness we hear more. We can listen to God's call in a sick parent, a confused student, a lonely stranger. Because the Lord is so patient with us, we begin to overcome our impatience with others. We can express Christian care and compassion with discretion, neither developing a savior complex nor neglecting the dedication expected of us. With God's help, it is possible to work hard and worry less. We can use our creative talents fully while tolerating our limits.

Perhaps it is God's will for us to remain in a service that is hidden, but it may also happen that we have to bear, as Christ did, the burden of public recognition and the consequent envy and jealousy it might arouse in others, to say nothing of the pride it could breed in us. Should this be the case, then our need is that much greater to imitate Jesus and retire occasionally to a desert oasis.

We cannot predict the consequences of our saying yes to his call. The life of the spirit involves risk. The desert is full of delight, but it is also at times the soul's dark night in which we cling, to quote St. John of the Cross, only to "dark faith." This faith then becomes the source of our hope and love. He wrote,

> . . . Just as faith is infused and rooted more deeply in the soul by means of that emptiness, darkness, and nakedness regarding all things . . . so too the charity of God is simultaneously infused and deeply rooted in the soul.[2]

All in all the desert is a great teacher. The people who go there are ordinary, as ordinary as those pilgrims I traveled with to Jerusalem. They have the same problems we do: their bills come due; their faucets leak; their children disappoint them; their employees complain; their health fails; their prayer life remains rather routine. They are ordinary people, who enjoy the carefreeness of youth, the responsibility of adulthood, the sobering reality of aging, the solitude of death. They are learning constantly about life from life itself.

Jesus knew who they were and so he taught them by using the kinds of lively stories they could understand. When he spoke, the people listened. He recounted in rich parables their hidden secrets, their fears, dreams, hopes, and desires. He called them his beloved. He offered them forgiveness. He told them how to combine daily labors with their inmost yearning for something more, for a meaning mere worldliness could not give. He showed them that the world was not an evil place but the Father's domain, his true delight. His spirit dwelt in every leaf and stone and sparrow. Most of all, he made his home in the hearts of *ordinary* people.

The Lord's love for us, his willingness to be the bridge of

2. Ibid., book 2, chapt. 24, p. 192.

reconciliation between sinful humanity and God, was realized in his incarnation, revealing as it does the divine plan of salvation. To carry this message further, he needed fervent, faithful disciples who would undergo their desert initiation and become living witnesses to faith in him.

This faith is the foundation of our spiritual life; it is the only proximate means to union with God. According to St. John of the Cross,

> . . . to be prepared for this divine union the intellect must be cleansed and emptied of everything relating to sense, divested and liberated of everything clearly apprehensible, inwardly pacified and silenced, and supported by faith alone, which is the only proximate and proportionate means to union with God.[3]

Like soldiers who have trained long and hard to carry out a difficult mission, so Jesus' disciples must go through the desert training of disciplining pride and its desperate clinging to pleasure, power, and possession, cut off from God. In the desert they learn to wait upon the Lord and to listen to his will in their daily situation. Sustained by grace, they become channels through which God calls the world out of darkness into the light of divinity.

The story of discipleship as a movement from desperation to delight is symbolized in Jesus' call of Levi, a tax collector (Mk. 2:13–14). Who could be more attached to the world in its worldliness than a man trained to manage its money? Yet it is to him that the Lord addressed his daring call, "Follow me." Without thinking, attending only to the faith that leapt into his heart, Levi said *yes!* This was clearly the right thing to do. He would not cease working; after all, he was a working man. He would simply leave one expression of his talent and assume another. Whereas before he had managed the affairs of men, he would now manage those of God for men.

3. Ibid., book 3, chapter 9, p. 129.

The Lord honored Levi in another way. He ate at his table with other tax collectors and laborers (Mk. 2:15–17). Known sinners joined him and his disciples for a good meal. Jesus welcomed them all. He taught them that they were children of the same Father. In his presence they felt that it was perhaps possible to reclaim their original calling. A sinner who repented could start with a clean slate. If the Lord said so, then it had to be true. If he had that much faith in them, they could begin to have some confidence in themselves. Far from giving up, they were being forgiven. He was inviting them to a new and hopeful life.

His teachings made good sense. He did not ask them to go off to some mountaintop but to stay in the desert of daily life while undergoing a change of heart. He seemed to say that conversion begins with a painful experience of desperation or repentance and ends with a delightful inward awareness of hope restored. Suddenly the noise of the world and its demands fades in importance. One wants only to listen to the voice of the Lord in silence. He speaks through our faith and formation tradition, and he speaks to us uniquely. What do we hear? How does this message affect our lifelong journey? Let us proceed slowly, silently, awaiting further revelation.

3

Silent Musings

Pause a while and know that I am God, exalted among the nations, exalted over the earth! (Ps. 46:10–11)

Silence. The word itself is soft, hushed, still. It has always attracted me, and I suspect the same is true for many people. Silence is more often than not a luxury hardly affordable but ardently desired. For as long as I can remember, I have not feared silence but welcomed it as a source of spiritual deepening. Like other people living in the world, I've grown accustomed to the noise in my place of work, to the raucous sounds of the city, to the inner disquiet stirred up by busy thoughts and earnest projects. Silence can be an escape from the functional responsibilities and physical demands of listening and conversing with colleagues, friends, and family members. But it can also be an opening to God.

In this atmosphere of outer and inner quiet, I can simply be myself before God. This experience is seldom lonely. Most often it is rich, full, life-giving. I envy those who hear mainly sounds emerging from nature—the ocean's swirl upon the shore, the sparrow's chatter in the trees, the wind swaying in the grass. These outer sounds, so natural, so free, seem to foster inner silence.

How agitating, by contrast, is the blare of rush-hour traffic, the din of crowded restaurants, the cries of curbside vendors. In a noise-polluted world it is even difficult to hear ourselves think, let alone try to be still and know God. Yet it seems essential for our spiritual life to seek some silence, no matter how busy we may be.

Silence is not to be shunned as empty space but to be befriended as fertile ground for intimacy with God. Spiritual masters, both Eastern and Western, point out that silence is a condition for being and remaining present to the Transcendent. Experience also confirms that silence fosters relaxation and may increase efficiency.

My days at the office can be terribly hectic. Tension mounts as the load of work increases. By day's end I feel drained. My neck may be stiff, my stomach cramped. I've learned to regard this tension as a signal to seek silence, if only for a short while. There are myriad ways to accomplish this goal. If we want something badly enough, we'll find a way to attain it. People living in the world need to be creative and innovative on this score, since they do not have silence built into their lives as a structure. Bells ring declaring silent times in monastic communities, but laypersons have no such helps. So how do we find time and space for silence?

The first step is to acknowledge our need for some quiet time. The second is to find practical ways to make this wish a reality. Many people rely on their cars to provide a place of silence. I know I do. The time spent driving to and from the office is time I set aside for silence: no radio, some attempt to still rambling thoughts, focusing only on the hum of tires along the road. A married couple I know created in their home what they call their silence room. They respect each other's need to go there at least once a day for ten or fifteen minutes of restorative stillness. Even the children are beginning to follow their example.

During these restful moments, I notice that before long the noise inside me begins to subside, and I start to feel relaxed. A few deep breaths, a long sigh, absorbed attentiveness to the silence, and life becomes bearable again. One may go for a quiet walk, enjoying the twilight hush between day and night. The tranquillity of nature slows us down and readies us for the silence of sleep with its refreshing, healing power.

This friendly bond between silence and the body is understandable, for our vital life began in the dense silence of our mother's womb. Imagine how still it was at our life's beginning. Will it not be as quiet when we experience our life's ending? How wondrous, how mysterious this final silence will be. Our lives open out like fresh blooms, only to be drawn toward this final closure. In some sense silence follows us from birth to death and beyond in the voiceless mystery of eternity.

Philosophers like Max Picard insist that silence is the mother of speech. Picard says that language becomes emaciated if it loses its bond with silence.[1] Silence protects speech, enabling us to communicate what is true and good. Silence prevents conversation from degenerating into idle chatter. Thomas Merton calls silence the mother of truth.[2] Picard also compares silence to a pregnant woman about to give birth,

1. See Max Picard, *The World of Silence,* trans. Stanley Godman (South Bend, Ind.: Gateway Editions, 1952), p. 15. Martin Heidegger also notes that only when we are silent can we be truly open for what is. See Michael Zimmerman, "Heidegger and Heraclitus on Spiritual Practice," *Philosophy Today* 27 (Summer 1983): 87–103. The bulk of this issue is devoted to "Soundings of Silence," current reviews of Bernard Dauenhauer's book, *Silence: The Phenomenon and Its Ontological Significance* (Bloomington, Ind.: Indiana Univ. Press, 1980).

2. See Thomas Merton, *Thoughts in Solitude* (Garden City, N.Y.: Doubleday & Co., Inc., Image Books, 1968), p. 84.

Silence is not static but generative insofar as it gives birth to true words.

If silence benefits the body, then it also aids effective functioning. For one thing, silence helps me to refocus my scattered attention. When my thoughts are back in order, I can better formulate what I want to say. Lacking silence, I'm likely to process information in piecemeal fashion. My mind starts to race, distractions dart in and out, and before long I lose my train of thought. I can hardly hold on to one idea before another rushes in.

A common problem, related to why we may seek to escape silence, is the discovery that it evokes nameless misgivings, guilt feelings, strange, disquieting anxiety. Anything is better than this mess, and so we flick on the radio or pick up the phone and talk to a friend. If we can pass through these initial fears and remain silent, we may experience a gradual waning of inner chaos. Silence becomes like a creative space in which we regain perspective on the whole.

Noise has the opposite effect. It tends to fragment us. We are inclined to focus on parts of the situation and to neglect the whole picture. Silence enables us to see all sides. I was interested to learn from a friend in corporate management that more and more board meetings begin with a mandated period of silence. The directors can then collect their thoughts and move toward clear-eyed decisions that take into account every possible dimension of a problem. Such clarity is more important than ever if executives are to anticipate the future and secure steady employment for their staffs. This is one more example of why silence is not a luxury for lay people but a spiritual necessity.

In silence the scattered pieces of my life fall into place, and I see again where I am going. Silence puts me in touch not only with the human spirit in all its richness, but also with the Holy Spirit. It opens me to the dimension of transcendence. I experience rest and peace. Stress and confusion, argument and anxiety, diminish in intensity. Silence becomes a sanctuary in which faith, hope, and love are restored. It readies me to listen to words that ring with eternal truth. Silence is almost like a psychic force that produces a heightened capacity for meditation, prayer, and contemplation.

The encounter between the soul and God ultimately transcends what language can contain. In many ways such intimacy is unspeakable. It is beyond words. In that silent center, where the Holy Spirit prays in our hearts, we transcend our bodily frailty as well as our functional limits. Neither seems to matter at such moments. Stilled, like a child on its mother's lap, we are with God and God is with us. He and I are wordlessly present to one another, yet a world of communication transpires between us. Because language cramps this reality, we fall silent. Words signifying human mastery dissolve as we listen to God's song. Tones we ordinarily miss due to life's rush are heard in silence. During such gratuitous moments, we are in tune with a silent treasure, God's presence in the core of our being.

This deep silence may not feel like much on the emotional level. It is not meant to produce spiritual highs. It simply warms our heart, and we know, without being able to prove why, that in the midst of the ups and downs of daily life we stand on the firm ground of God's unchanging love. He assures us of this love not in flashes of lightning or furious thunder but in soft, gentle breezes (1 K. 19:13). We wait upon God in these gifted moments as he waits upon us. We feel at one with the Mother of Christ, who silently listened to the angel and then gave her consent to bear God's Word in the flesh.

Silence thus touches every sphere of our existence. It brings to our bodies the grace of relaxation, to our minds the benefit of increased attention. It makes possible thoughtful speech and leads to more reflective action. Most of all it enables us to be centered in God. Its practical implications for formation are obvious, since it is a founding principle of the spiritual life.

Everyone needs silence: the teacher, the nurse, the social worker; the artist, the poet, the doctor; the lawyer, the house-wife, the cabdriver. To neglect this need is to risk living a tense, fragmented, spiritless life. Formation in Christian living is not confined to monasteries; it is a survival measure in the modern world. If we do not nourish our souls, they atrophy as do bodies without food. To maintain any kind of Christlike presence in the world, we need to seek silence and its fruits in the practices of spiritual reading, meditation, prayer, and con-templation.

Because we are made in the form and likeness of God, we must ready ourselves for his visitation. When we least expect it, in the ordinary routines of our life, he may make his pres-ence known. Are we silent enough to hear his voice? Can we welcome him into hearts stilled and waiting, or do noisy dis-tractions block the way? His words say:

> Look, I am standing at the door, knocking. If one of you hears me calling and opens the door, I will come in to share his meal, side by side with him. Those who prove victorious I will allow to share my throne, just as I was victorious myself and took my place with my Father on his throne. If anyone has ears to hear, let him listen to what the Spirit is saying . . . (Rv. 3:20–22)

It does not matter to God which house we inhabit. He stands at the door and knocks. We can hear his tapping only if we live in silence. Silence is God's special instrument. He uses it like a harpist reaches for heavenly chords to say things to us that are beyond words.

I remember a priest telling me of an experience he had with a severely ill parishioner, who had been hospitalized for some time. When he met her she was inconsolable. Ever since she had been admitted for care, she had been unable to pray. This was an immense shock to her, for all of her life she had been a believer in daily prayer. The priest visited her regularly and offered what help he could, but her inability to pray persisted. Finally, he asked her to tell him as clearly as possible how she prayed. She said she mainly talked to God. Now, when she tried to do so, she became choked up, angry, disgusted with life. The priest advised her to try saying nothing to the Lord, simply to remain silent, as Jesus did before his accusers. Suddenly the lady started weeping. It was as if his words had taken from her the burden of having to talk to God. She could be quiet in his presence. She could allow her pent-up emotions to gush out in silence, without trying to analyze what she was feeling. It was impossible to understand fully all that he was asking of her anyway, so why not be still and listen? Only silence proved to be an empty enough space to contain her feelings about life and pending death.

If we love truth, we will be lovers of silence. So say the words of the Syrian monk Isaac of Nineveh:

> Many are avidly seeking but they alone find who remain in continual silence . . . Every man who delights in a multitude of words, even though he says admirable things, is empty within. If you love truth, be a lover of silence. Silence like the sunlight will illuminate you in God and will deliver you from the phantoms of ignorance. Silence will unite you to God himself . . . [3]

Words of power like these flow from a wellspring of silence. They ready us to listen to the wisdom found in scripture and in the writings of the spiritual masters, a wisdom that teaches us how to integrate daily life with divinely inspired revelations embedded in spoken and written words.

3. Quoted by Thomas Merton in *Contemplative Prayer* (New York: Herder and Herder, 1969), p. 33.

4

Words of Power

A child of God listens to the words of God . . . (Jn. 8:47)

One of the most moving scenes in the film of Helen Keller's life, *The Miracle Worker,* occurs when her teacher makes her touch water flowing from a pump and simultaneously connect what she touches with the word "water." This is the miracle both have been anticipating, for to name something is to begin to know it. For a potential scholar like Helen the words she rapidly assimilates after that are full of wonder. Through them she is able to live a normal life of listening, reading, and speaking in accordance with the limits of her deafness and blindness. Curiously her *disability* releases a lecturing *ability* seldom surpassed.

Words are sources of new life, as when a child learns to speak or a foreigner masters a language other than his or her native tongue. Words can destroy people, as in the case of false propaganda, sly insinuation, spiteful insult. As St. James says,

"We use [the tongue] to bless the Lord and Father, but we also use it to curse men who are made in God's image: the blessing and the curse come out of the same mouth" (Jm. 3:9–10).

Words are essential for our faith formation. To be a child of God we must listen to God's words in revelation and live the best way we can in accordance with their directives. The parables, examples, symbols, and images Jesus uses to convey his message contain an inexhaustible depth of meaning. That is why we never tire of hearing them. They embody a wisdom no human mind could disclose, and hence their impact will last forever. One generation hands them on to the next, thus assuring the continuity of our Christian heritage.

Like Christ we may offer suffering others a word of consolation, reminding them to trust in the loving providence of God. We help one another through words of encouragement and, should it be necessary, through words of admonition. Words can be pointers to the Transcendent when they draw us closer to the numinous, infinite wellspring of beauty shining through our otherwise dismal world. We share the Lord's words in our joy and in our pain, for faith grows in light and darkness. We need only to witness the public ministry and passion of Jesus to know that his words are an expression of his life. There is no separation between what he says and who he is. Hence his words are full of power. To read and believe in them heightens our awareness of God's love as it sustains us in everyday life.

The texts of scripture, the commentaries and autobiographies of the spiritual masters, encourage us to see ourselves and others, things and events, as God's gift. This reverent stance permeates our attitudes and actions. Directives pertaining to love of neighbor become motivating guidelines for our spiritual life. We are less inclined to focus on competition and acquisition as matters of ultimate importance and more intent on cultivating the inner dedication needed to serve others.

Like a drill tests layers of earth to determine if they will yield oil, so we let these words tap into and release the natural treasure of our love and longing for God. We cannot remain indifferent to this force of love in the core of our being. The Christ-life within should stir our thoughts and affections. His words are not pieces of information but doorways to Christian formation. They help us to know, appraise, and embrace the unique and communal destiny the Lord wants us to pursue.

If his words are to evoke this kind of response, we must read them in the right frame of mind. It is important to move from an information-gathering approach, which tends to master the text, to a docile approach, which readies us for graced transformation. This movement from mastery to discipleship creates a sphere of mutuality between us and the text. Transcendent meanings can only be released when we establish a personal relationship with these words, thereby allowing them to touch and possibly to change our life.

This relational bonding between the listening heart of the reader and the words of power in the text is characterized by at least three attitudes: receptivity, appreciation, and participation. We could compare this kind of reading to what happens when we meet a friend. Our presence to one another is spontaneously receptive. We don't have to think about how much we enjoy being together. We are simply there for one another. Similarly, the affinity we feel is rooted in our deep appreciation for one another's uniqueness. We respect each other physically, psychologically, spiritually. This appreciative mood makes us eager to listen to one another and to draw forth further insights from our conversation. Last, but not least, we genuinely care about one another. We want to be part of each other's life, not outsiders looking in, but truly involved and concerned persons. We are for one another because we know in some mysterious way that we participate in a love that is totally for us.

Formative reading means, therefore, being receptive to those directives in the text that touch our heart and evoke inner longings to receive God's word as the center of our life. We appreciate the timeless meanings of the Lord's message, while gently letting go of time-bound accretions. What we seek are points with which we can positively resonate, not ones that spark argumentation. Rather than rebuff the text because we feel a few resistances, we try, as in a good relationship, to work these through via further reflection. Most of all, we attempt to make that with which we resonate a real part of our life. This means that we not only imbibe inner attitudes conducive to living a Christian spirituality in the world, but we also let these attitudes flow forth in daily actions. Our stance toward the text is not that of a spectator upon transcendent reality but of a participant in it.

Formative reading thus involves a shift, in Adrian van Kaam's terms, from "form-giving," in which we are inclined to impose our meaning on the text, to "form-receiving," in which we let its meaning influence us. We move from a mainly argumentative, rationalistic, faultfinding mentality to an appreciative, meditative, confirming mood. Our spiritual life is refreshed whenever we take time to savor these timeless values. They become a living part of who we are. The text is like a bridge between the limits of our life here and now and the possibilities awaiting us if we open our minds and hearts to God.

Relating to sacred words in this way is like holding a two-edged sword (Heb. 4:12). The Lord's words challenge us to look again at the quality and seriousness of our Christian life. At times his words cut deep into our heart. We behold the spectre of living a superficial spirituality and feel the pinch of compunction. Are we merely putting on a holy front, or is our life really lived in union with God? The words we read compel us to take off the mask of worldly sophistication and to admit that without God we are and can do nothing.

The words of the Lord are like rain from heaven. They quench our thirst for truth in a wholly satisfying way. God himself is at work in this reader-text relationship. He uses the text to facilitate our inner transformation. When words touch and transform our heart, we can be sure he is the artist behind them. He plants the seed of the word in our soil, whether it is parched or fertile. After a time of germination, it begins to bear the lasting fruit of divine transformation. We move from indifference to rededication, from casual prayer to transcendent presence.

Formative reading could thus be defined as the art of listening with inner ears of faith to what God is saying in the happenings that comprise our life. The fourteenth-century English mystic Julian of Norwich illustrates what I mean. Julian believed with all her heart that God never ceases to look after us. She chose two striking images to validate his providential love and protection: one of clothing, the other of a hazelnut. Of the first her words say:

> He is our clothing, for he is that love which wraps and enfolds us, embraces us and guides us, surrounds us for his love, which is so tender that he may never desert us. And so in this sight I saw truly that he is everything which is good, as I understand.[1]

The second image is equally tender.

> And in this he showed me something small, no bigger than a hazelnut, lying in the palm of my hand, and I perceived that it was as round as any ball. I looked at it and thought: What can this be? And I was given this general answer: It is everything which is made. I was amazed that it could last, for I thought that it was so little that it could suddenly fall into nothing. And I was answered in my understanding: It lasts and always will,

1. Julian of Norwich, *Showings*, trans. Edmund Colledge, O.S.A., and James Walsh, S.J., in *The Classics of Western Spirituality* (New York: Paulist Press, 1978), p. 130.

because God loves it; and thus everything has being through the love of God.[2]

Whatever Julian saw became a manifestation of God's loving kindness. His words, so full of power and promise, can be applied by extension to every situation, to pain as well as to prosperity. Affliction is as much a part of life as consolation and delight. Julian received the confirmation she sought that God's purpose is operable at all times, that nothing occurs by chance. All is done in accordance with his "prescient wisdom."[3] For this reason she was "compelled to admit that everything which is done is done well, for our Lord God does everything."[4]

This spirit of faith springs from the conviction that God himself, through the cross and resurrection of Christ, will in some mysterious way bring our life ultimately to union with him. Julian's faith did not reside in naive optimism, but in a direct showing from the Lord during a sequence of intense mystical experiences. He revealed to her his deep care for our well-being, his desire to grant us the fullness of peace and joy, glimpsed in this life and guaranteed to the faithful in eternity.

Julian's vision that "all will be well" confirmed her trust in God's power of transformation. The way he turns sadness to joy and darkness to light accounted for her gladness, caught jubilantly in this text.

> . . . I learned that it is more honour to God to know everything in general than it is to take delight in any special thing. And if I were to act wisely, in accordance with this teaching, I should not be glad because of any special thing or be greatly distressed by anything at all, for all will be well; for the fulness of joy is to contemplate God in everything.[5]

2. Ibid., p. 130.
3. Ibid., p. 197.
4. Ibid., p. 197.
5. Ibid., pp. 236–37.

The writing of the eighteenth-century spiritual director Jean-Pierre de Caussade validates Julian's faith. His main condition for reading God's word and applying it to daily life was abandonment to divine providence. This surrendered stance enables us to perceive God's appearance in "the sacrament of the present moment."[6] According to de Caussade,

> there is never a moment when God does not come forward in the guise of some suffering or some duty, and all that takes place within us, around us and through us both includes and hides his activity. Yet, because it is invisible, we are always taken by surprise and do not recognize his operation until it has passed by us. If we could lift the veil and if we watched with vigilant attention, God would endlessly reveal himself to us and we should see and rejoice in his active presence in all that befalls us.[7]

De Caussade's words insist that God is with us at every moment. His revelations go on uninterrupted. If only we could lift the veil of worldly preoccupation and watch with vigilant attention, God would endlessly reveal himself to us. We would see his epiphany in the most mundane appearances. How is this possible? De Caussade's words respond emphatically:

> It is faith which interprets God for us. Without its light we should not even know that God was speaking, but would hear only the confused, meaningless babble of creatures. As Moses saw the flame of fire in the bush and heard the voice of God coming from it, so faith will enable us to understand his hidden signs, so that amidst all the apparent clutter and disorder we shall see all the loveliness and perfection of divine wisdom.[8]

Such faith transforms the way we live. Through its power to reveal the invisible order of reality, we see that "every moment

6. Jean-Pierre de Caussade, *Abandonment to Divine Providence,* trans. John Beevers (Garden City, N.Y.: Doubleday & Co., Inc., Image Books, 1975), p. 16.
7. Ibid., p. 36.
8. Ibid., p. 37.

is crammed with invisible riches."[9] We know from experience the simple yet profound truth that "each moment contains some sign of the will of God."[10] In the light of faith, we learn how to read these holy messages. Through the grace of Christ, we become disciples who can "draw upon that will veiled and hidden beneath every little detail of our lives . . ."[11]

This capacity to make connections between the text being read and our current situation can become a distinguishing feature of our life in the world. We not only absorb words and submit them to the reasoning process, but we allow these words to evoke personal symbols, stories, memories, and anticipations. Significant connections may coalesce in our imagination and reveal meanings that were previously hidden. Amidst clutter and disorder, we suddenly behold the "loveliness and perfection of divine wisdom."[12]

Such reading makes us wonder if we are responding creatively to God's will or merely waiting for our own expectations to be fulfilled. Will we despair in the face of life's limits or welcome them as challenging opportunities? Are we able to see our past, present, and future in the light of God's benevolence? A first step in the right direction is to personalize once again the ageless wisdom embedded in these words of power. Reading and rereading them will help us to find the elusive link between life experience and the living God.

9. Ibid., p. 40.
10. Ibid., p. 40.
11. Ibid., p. 41.
12. Ibid., p. 37.

5

Formative Reading

Heaven and earth will pass away, but my words will never pass away. (Lk. 21:33)

The implications of this text are awesome. If everything passes away, if only his words remain, then surely we cannot survive without reading and following them. Christians, to be sure, are a little flock, but they have heard God's word revealed in Holy Scripture. As his followers, we know that the call to holiness is extended to each member of his family, from beggars to ballerinas, from handicapped persons to physicians, from mechanics to merchants. His mercy rests upon the physically poor as well as the spiritually impoverished. His peace extends from our own shores to the entire planet. His justice embraces every person, whatever the skin color or the shape of clothing. All have the right to live decent, unoppressed lives in the world he has given to us. We believe that this earth is not ours to exploit or to destroy. It is the house of God, which he asks us to tend for his sake, saying through St. Paul:

> . . . You are no longer aliens or foreign visitors: you are citizens like all the saints, and part of God's household. You are part of a building that has the apostles and prophets for its foundations, and Christ Jesus himself for its main cornerstone. As every structure is aligned on him, all grow into one holy temple in the Lord; and you too, in him, are being built into a house where God lives, in the Spirit. (Ep. 2:19–22)

In our day many try by human efforts alone to solve the problems of our planet. Ironically our success, cut off from a living sense of God's presence, now threatens to annihilate us. Perhaps the time has come to reawaken the sleeping giant of Christian spirituality and its rich literary tradition, which teaches us how to foster a life of holiness while recognizing that such a gift is ultimately only God's to give.

Formative reading challenges us to listen with docility to spiritual directives found in texts of lasting value.[1] We temper the busy train of thoughts that rush through our working day in order to dwell with texts that arouse our longing for God. Such reading, done in a slowed-down way on a regular basis, reestablishes our commitment to Christ while helping us to let go of peripheral concerns.

Formative reading is generally uplifting, but these gratuitous moments are not guaranteed. The danger is that we may grow discouraged if nothing happens. A student of mine told me that reading St. Teresa of Avila's autobiography kept her going during a period of intense aridity. St. Teresa's need for a book at such times paralleled her own experience.

> . . . It seems to me that it was the Lord's providence that I did not find anyone to instruct me, for, on account of my being

1. For an extensive treatment of the topic of formative reading, the obstacles to this practice, and the conditions for it, one can consult my books beginning with *Approaching the Sacred*. Of special interest for this chapter is the text entitled *A Practical Guide to Spiritual Reading*. These references can be found in the bibliography that accompanies this book.

unable as I say to reflect discursively, it would have been impossible, I think, to have persevered for the eighteen years I suffered this trial, and in that great dryness. In all those years, except for the time after Communion, I never dared to begin prayer without a book.[2]

If we rely too much on affective feelings, we may forget St. Teresa's insight that union with God is more a matter of willing the good than of merely feeling consoled.

God asks us to remain faithful to his words in all circumstances, even if our human minds can never fully understand their meaning, even if our actions fail at times to conform to our beliefs. He conceals the mystery of his message from the worldly wise but not from mere children. In addressing the Corinthians, St. Paul attempted to articulate this paradox:

> Take yourselves, for instance, brothers, at the time when you were called: how many of you were wise in the ordinary sense of the word, how many were influential people, or came from noble families? No, it was to shame the wise that God chose what is foolish by human reckoning, and to shame what is strong that he chose what is weak by human reckoning; those whom the world thinks common and contemptible are the ones that God has chosen—those who are nothing at all to show up those who are everything. The human race has nothing to boast about to God, but God has made you members of Christ Jesus and by God's doing he has become our wisdom, and our virtue, and our holiness, and our freedom. (1 Co. 1:26–31)

The Lord himself compared the kingdom to a buried treasure "hidden in a field which someone has found; he hides it again, goes off happy, sells everything he owns and buys the field" (Mt. 13:44). This parable is baffling by worldly standards. If a person finds a treasure, the usual inclination would

2. *The Collected Works of St. Teresa of Avila,* vol. 1, *The Book of Her Life,* trans. Kieran Kavanaugh, O.C.D., and Otilio Rodriguez, O.C.D. (Washington, D.C.: Institute of Carmelite Studies, ICS Publications, 1976), p. 44.

be to squander it immediately, whereas the person in the parable reburied it. There are many meanings to this story, but one occurs to me in reference to formative reading. Finding the treasure is like finding a text that profoundly touches my soul. I want to hide this meaning in my heart and ponder it for a while in the light of the whole field of my spiritual life. To discover this direction, I would be happy to let go of other preoccupations, to sell what I *own* in order to buy the field where I *am*.

Reading texts as mysterious as these parables of the kingdom is comparable to the eastern practice of puzzling a koan.[3] This is a question basically impossible to answer, or a sentence defying human logic, that the teacher gives to his disciple. The master is not interested in his solving the puzzle rationally. His intention is that the disciple live in wonder. Information is of no help here. If the message were decipherable, the disciple would take pride in his cleverness, thus missing the whole point of the exercise. It is to foster humility and to learn that the gift of enlightenment is beyond one's control.

Similarly, formative reading of scripture can lead one to texts that baffle logic while validating experience. For instance, Jesus told his followers that

> the kingdom of heaven is like a mustard seed which a man took and sowed in his field. It is the smallest of all the seeds, but when it has grown it is the biggest shrub of all and becomes a tree so that the birds of the air come and shelter in its branches. (Mt. 13:31–32)

3. For an explanation and illustration of this eastern technique, see William Johnston, S.J., *Christian Zen* (New York: Harper & Row Publishers, Inc., 1971), especially pp. 57–67. According to another author, Michael Zimmerman, a Zen koan is comparable to an *aporia,* a term the Greeks used to describe a knotty puzzle that demanded unusual insight. In Zen, he says, "koan-work is designed to bring the aspirant to the point of rational breakdown so that the breakthrough to alternative experience becomes available." See his article "Heidegger and Heraclitus on Spiritual Practice," *Philosophy Today* 27 (Summer 1983): 98.

How paradoxical that a seed so small should yield such a majestic tree, yet how many times is this experience validated in scripture? The Lord told Abram, who was childless, "Look up to heaven and count the stars if you can. Such will be your descendants . . ." (Gn. 15:5). God makes the impossible possible. This paradox may generate mental anguish, but, by the same token, it opens us to the mystery of the Sacred. Humanly, we are incapable of understanding God's essence, but we can behold his appearance in our daily life and follow his words. This listening is not a question of logical analysis but of abiding with God in faith, hope, and love.

As disciples of the word, we remain gently open to divine directives. We focus our attention on the text at hand and let it speak to our here and now situation. Simultaneously, we abide with the text and apply its meaning wherever possible to our lives. We purposefully set aside time, slow down, and read reflectively. We may even mark whatever in the text evokes a spontaneous resonance and ask ourselves why we feel this way. In the course of time, after persistent practice of this spiritual exercise, we may find the words taking on a life of their own inside us. Their wisdom sinks into our heart and affects our thoughts and actions. We want to share the fruits of this transformation with others in need of inspiration, with our children, our fellow parishioners, our colleagues and students.

In this way we experience the passage from reading to meditation to action. To read is to receive the word into the heart; to meditate is to listen to its deeper meaning; to act implies a silent exchange of love in which I know that the Lord is the source of my strength. Relaxed and refreshed by these experiences, I can return to the task at hand, be it parenting, parish programming, teaching, or a combination of all three.

As we increase our attentiveness to sacred texts, new ranges of significance light up. The text stimulates us to go beyond superficial interpretations. We learn to wait upon the word, rereading a text of depth several times. The older we grow, the more meanings we are likely to detect. We accept that in this matter of holiness God does not conform to our time frame. So we wait in gentle anticipation for lights to emerge. We ask God to help us reach ever deeper levels of wisdom, whenever and however he chooses to grant this gift.

In the last of his completed sermons on the *Song of Songs,* St. Bernard of Clairvaux reflected:

> . . . This secret remains hidden from the wise and the cautious, and is revealed to the little ones. Yes, my brothers, it is great, it is great and sublime, the virtue of humility which obtains the reality of what cannot be taught. It alone is worthy to receive from the Word and to conceive through the Word what it cannot explain in words.[4]

Humility opens our inner ears. It enables us to acknowledge the truth of who we are and who God is. Only the humble can understand the deep resonance of God's voice in the whole of creation. Humility withstands any arrogant tendency to reduce the word to our purposes. When we live in humble presence, God may reveal to us while we read insights that transcend human expectations.

Humility makes possible this playful interchange between us and God that is full of surprises. The path along which the spiritual writers lead us is seldom smooth by human standards, for it is the way of the cross. It is the path of suffering, of unpopularity, of imitating a person who by the world's measure was a scandal. Jesus did not start a political revolution or build communes to house the destitute of Jerusalem. Though he did not write a book, countless men and women have risked their lives for the sake of his word. He does not mitigate the condition for the possibility of following him.

4. Quoted by Jean Leclercq, O.S.B., in *The Love of Learning and the Desire for God: A Study of Monastic Culture,* trans. Catherine Misrahi (New York: Fordham Univ. Press, 1961), p. 329.

If anyone wants to be a follower of mine, let him renounce himself and take up his cross and follow me. For anyone who wants to save his life will lose it; but anyone who loses his life for my sake, and for the sake of the gospel will save it. What gain, then, is it for a man to win the whole world and ruin his life? (Mk. 8:34–37)

Each person must ask: Am I willing to abide by these words? Will I let them become the guiding directive of my life? In these and similar texts, the life of discipleship unfolds with all its joy and suffering. The words of St. John the Baptist become our own: "He must increase, while I must decrease" (Jn. 3:30).

God expects us to cooperate with his grace by forsaking our definitions of what our life as laity in the Church should be like, of how it should turn out. He is writing the text of our life's plan; our task is to read it. We may lose the way once in a while, but he awakens us through formative reading, for

the Lord Yahweh has given me a disciple's tongue. So that I may know how to reply to the wearied he provides me with speech. Each morning he wakes me to hear, to listen like a disciple. The Lord Yahweh has opened my ear. For my part, I made no resistance neither did I turn away. (Is. 50:4–5)

As long as we hear his voice and continue to obey him, God will show us how to rouse ourselves and others to a life of reflection, prayer, and service. He will enlighten our minds and stir our hearts so that we may know him more and more intimately, that we may understand and feel more vividly our call to praise and serve him in this world. He will teach us how to order our whole life in accordance with his holy will.

The way of formative reading is the way of discipleship, of following Christ more faithfully in this world that we may enjoy his company forever in the next. With St. Paul we too can say:

. . . I have not yet won, but am still running, trying to capture the prize for which Christ Jesus captured me. I can assure you . . . I am far from thinking that I have already won. All I can say is that I forget the past and I strain ahead for what is still to come; I am racing for the finish, for the prize to which God calls us upward to receive in Christ Jesus . . . If there is some point on which you see things differently, God will make it clear to you; meanwhile, let us go forward on the road that has brought us to where we are. (Ph. 3:12–16)

For us, going forward means moving from formative reading to further meditation on the meaning of God's call heard day by day in the mundane events that make up our life in the world.

6

Moving into Meditation

If you love listening you will learn, if you lend an ear, wisdom will be yours. (Si. 6:33–34)

This text confirms a long-standing intuition of the masters that listening is the doorway to divine wisdom. The meditative stance is not a matter of imposing our thoughts on reality but of attending in quiet vigilance, in gentle reverence, to what is there. Listening reminds us that spiritual formation is first of all a question of receptivity. We cannot give to others what has not already been given to us.

To listen, as the text of Sirach suggests, is to receive learning. To lend an ear to our spiritual teachers, texts, and traditions is to be granted the gift of wisdom. Moving into meditation does not mean imposing preconceived notions on reality; it does not imply puzzling the God problem until we find a reasonable solution.

Listening means being released from willfulness, arrogance, and self-assertiveness. It calls for respectful presence to the mystery we are meditating, for humble openness to its meaning. Such listening or apprehending is prior to our appraisal of these meanings and our decision to incorporate them into our spiritual development, should God give us the grace for this growth.

Let us look more fully at the art of listening, for this art alone enables us to move forward in meditative thinking. Listening is only possible to the degree that we let go of the grip of our egotistic will and become inwardly and outwardly silent, alert, receptive, attentive. Then we may be able to think clearly or meditate; it becomes possible to reflect on our lives as a whole or on a text we are reading. What we hear sinks from our minds into our hearts. Ideas are not exploited to serve our purposes but to direct us to deeper wisdom, to a revelation of persons, events, and things as they are in themselves. We become the servants rather than the masters of the word.

Often the act of meditation or thinking is equated with judging, comparing, evaluating, categorizing. These are legitimate functions of the rational ego or of what many today call our computer intelligence. Such thinking is scientific, logically consistent, methodological. It is directed toward managing life reasonably well, getting chaos under control. This thinking is absolutely necessary at times, though of its nature it is more informative than formative.

Were we to characterize the informative approach to meditation, we might say it is progressive, or linear: one thought builds upon another. It holds feelings at bay, lest one become too subjective and lose the logical line. It is intellectually stimulating, argumentative, even calculative. It prizes highly the witty winning of a point, the disclosure of clever concepts, the imparting of new facts.

Informative thinking moves us rather quickly away from experience toward conceptual control. Examples, stories, parables seem to get in the way of intellectual clarification. They appear to clutter up our line of thought. The outcome of such thinking is often reducible to a diagram, chart, or graph or to a concise answer.

Complementing the informative approach, and equally, if not essentially, important for spiritual deepening, is the way of formative thinking.[1] This approach is more dwelling, repetitive, circular. It spirals down to deeper layers of meaning rather than move from point to point. It brings us home to our experiential life as we move from head to heart.

Formative thinking or reflective meditation encourages us to surrender to the mystery of life we cannot master. It enables us to return to the homeland of transcendent formation, to truths of spiritual unfolding that are eternal, like love, trust, humility, compassion. Such thinking does not set out to accomplish something but simply to be somewhere: with this poem, this prayer, this paragraph.

The spiral approach often inspires us, that is, it breathes forth and breeds spirit-filled thoughts in the center of our heart. We are mindful of the mystery of everydayness, of the gifts embedded in the simplest experiences, like smelling a rose. We want to stay with these things, to mine their meaning, to be affected by them.

Formative thinking is full of examples, stories, symbols, images, metaphors, parables. This is the "stuff" real meditation is made of because it contains much more than any word or concept could express. Experience can never be exhausted by informative thought; there is always more to be said. That is why we can read the same text several times and still derive inspiration and new insights from it.

1. "Formative thinking is a type of thinking that relates directly or proximately to our formation." Further analysis of the distinction between these two modes of thinking is found in Adrian van Kaam, *Fundamental Formation,* vol. 1, *Formative Spirituality* (New York: Crossroad Publishing Co., 1983), pp. xvii–xix.

Life, thought about formatively, is a never-ending source of wonder and meaning. Such thinking, as the philosopher Martin Heidegger might say, is a mode of thanking, of loving, of just being. The informative thinker seeks to do or to accomplish; the formative thinker intends only to become more fully engaged in life.[2] He or she knows that there is always more to learn, the greatest lesson being that our egos do not control our destiny; God does.

Learning to meditate reflectively is not easy for the Western mind. We are accustomed to dominating things; we don't like the idea that they are there to teach us. But if we don't love listening, we will never learn, and wisdom will forever elude us. At issue here is not the destruction of the ego or the diminishment of our gifts of logical intelligence. Our only concern is that we remain open and receptive to more than what the scattering ego finds important.

Take the experience of just sitting and being open to what presents itself.[3] Most Westerners would scoff at such an experience or secretly fear they could not sustain it without becoming fidgety or nervous. They would ask, "What's the use of it anyway?" The label "navel gazing" may be applied and lead to the end of reflective listening/seeing/being.

Why do we resist these moments? They can and do provoke anxiety, for what discloses itself is not submissive to our will. What reveals itself, according to Michael Zimmerman, is "the groundlessness and mortality of human life."

> Deciding to listen requires a kind of leap, a letting-go into the abyss, a real starting-over without guarantees. With this leap however, our "thinking" is not at an end but at the beginning

2. See Michael Zimmerman, "Heidegger and Heraclitus on Spiritual Practice," *Philosophy Today* 27 (Summer 1983): 93.

3. I am indebted not only to Michael Zimmerman for these ideas but also to Frederick Franck, *The Zen of Seeing: Seeing/Drawing as Meditation* (New York: Random House Inc., Vintage Trade Books, 1973).

. . . Those who have never made the venture of "just thinking" know as little about it as the blind person knows about colors. Yet the paradox of human existence is that we blind ourselves; we try to cover up the openness that we always already are. Our flight from our own mortal openness will never succeed in preventing death, but it can lead to death in life. Otto Rank once remarked that the neurotic person is one "who refused the loan (life) in order to avoid the payment of the debt (death)." Fully to live requires that we let go into the anxiety that calls us back to life, so that living is as intense as is our friendship with our mortality.[4]

It is clear that meditative thinking or formative reflection flows from our hearing of the word and our listening to its transcendent meaning. Such spiritual practice is a prelude to our hearing again in prayer. Before our prayer can become more contemplative, we need to become better practitioners of formative thinking, for it trains us to let go and to let God be Lord and Master of our lives.

Practically speaking, are there some guidelines we can follow that move us into this kind of meditation? These guidelines presuppose that we have developed and are developing three intertwining attitudes: awe for the mystery of formation in universe, humanity, and history; appreciation of life as a gift full of meaning if we but open our hearts to God's call; and appraisal of our direction and destiny in accordance with his providential plan.[5] In this regard, some people may welcome the opportunity to have regular talks with a spiritual director or confessor.

The first guideline is to calm down my whole self, physically, psychologically, spiritually. Too many people in the

4. Zimmerman, pp. 93–94.
5. These attitudes and dispositions are more fully developed in a series of glossary definitions and descriptions published by Adrian van Kaam in the journal *Studies in Formative Spirituality* 1–4, 1980–83, published by the Institute of Formative Spirituality, Duquesne University, Pittsburgh, Pa. 15282.

world live life in the fast lane. They seem to be always in a rush. Pocket calendars and digital clocks dominate their existence. Meditation means moving into the slow lane for a while. It requires slowing down to listen, to see, to ruminate upon a text that touches one's heart.

Times set aside for meditation or reflective reading invite us gradually to let go of all that preoccupies our clockwork minds so that we can relax in the presence of the Transcendent. It may take a while to quiet down, as the nervous tapping of our fingers or the twitching of our lips may indicate. A few deep breaths will help. We might also engage in some active relaxation exercises, like tightening and unclenching our hands, arms, and shoulders.[6] A few rolls of the neck may unkink that part of the anatomy.

Once we relax physically, it may be more obvious how spastically distracted we are psychologically and mentally. No sooner do we try to attend appreciatively to nature or a text than a veritable kaleidoscope of thoughts rushes in like flies in an open pantry. The more we try to swat them, the thicker the cloud becomes. These thoughts are like waves on the surface of the sea. The important thing is not to pay attention to them.

Meditation dips below surface analysis and its distracting demands. It opens us to a deeper realm of consciousness wherein we feel calm and present to the wonder of reality as a diver experiences the quiet depths of the sea. We can use as our diving gear to go to that still bottom one word or one phrase softly repeated. More and more we will find ourselves drawn toward the mystery in whom all is sourced, ourselves included.

The calming down stage readies us as the agents or subjects of meditation. It is what we do to get ready for this spiritual exercise. Choosing the object or kind of meditation we shall engage in is the second guideline. We could use our time of

6. Practical instructions for these exercises are found in Herbert Benson, *The Relaxation Response* (New York: William Morrow & Co., 1975).

meditation to do nothing but be present to a flower, a forest, a mountain range, a sunset. This is nature meditation. We could focus peacefully on a concept we want to understand better and allow new insights to emerge. This is focal meditation. We could also dwell upon a text of our choice, rereading it and ruminating upon it. This is reading meditation, which, when done with liturgical texts or the Bible, is called *lectio divina.* It is formative reading carried into the stage of personalized reflection. It is a spiritual practice I recommend highly for people in the world, since it not only slows us down and helps us to be more attentive, but it also teaches us a great deal about our faith. Overall it is an excellent aid to ongoing formation.

That being the case, let us look at this mode of meditation a little more closely, for it draws us out of mediocre Christianity toward intimacy with God, who uses such words to call us home to union with him. When a text touches us with any degree of intensity, it invites us to lift our eyes from the page we are reading and meditate on its meaning. The text, so to speak, gives us a morsel of good food to chew upon. We want to discover why this is a word for our life, why we resonate with it or feel resistance. We want to linger over its meaning, as emerging in the context of our current situation.

The text may lead us to assess our failings but, equally important, it affirms our strengths. As we reflect upon this message, we may note the appearance in our mind's eye of a fuller picture of ourselves. We become more familiar with the person Christ is calling us to be. In these moments of receiving insight from a text, we sense God's self-communication to us. We know that he is using the text to touch our hearts as well as to stimulate our minds. Meditation frees us from having to conform instantly to a model of perfection. We realize that we are involved in a long process of becoming who we most deeply are.

When we meditate on the inspired words of scripture, we

may feel as if we are being drawn in two directions at once. On the one side, we are impelled upward by the transcendent mystery of Christ's lordship and love for us. On the other side, we are moved by our human vulnerability, by how far away we seem to be from the goal of consonant Christian formation.

We seem to forget that it is exactly our brokenness and sin that Christ chose to overcome. Because he took on our human condition, we can trust that he understands our weakness and does transform it. The more we acknowledge our dependency on the Lord, the more we can let go of useless projects of self-salvation and listen to the voice of the Holy Spirit speaking in our human spirit.

Because we are meditating on a given text, there is less danger of becoming absorbed in ourselves. Though we may become more aware of our sinfulness, anger, and guilt, we are simultaneously called into the transcendent circle of forgiveness, gentleness, compassion. The text becomes a friendly companion, reminding us of the infinite range of God's mercy. We can let go of the craving, possessive, arrogant side of ourselves and become children cherished by God.

The third and final guideline pertaining to meditation is linked to our response, namely, we have to move from intellectualizing about a concept or a text to personalizing it in relation to our here and now life. Meditation is meant to affect us, to change and transform our heart. It challenges our current assumptions, opinions, prejudices. By lessening tension and opening us to the transcendent, it moves us forward into an harmonious life of prayer, contemplation, and service.

In the light of this third guideline, regarding the embodiment in daily life of the material meditated upon, we can suggest the following results for people in the world. We will definitely begin to live a more Christ-centered life, based on the revealed and practiced truths, teachings, and traditions of the Church. We will experience richer ranges of imagination, thought, decision, and action, in keeping with our calling to transform the world into the house of God.

We shall listen more astutely to his voice in everyday demands rather than only expecting to hear it in dramatic events. We shall be more patient during times of dryness, knowing that God appears to true believers in desert places. Above all, we shall become more refined instruments of God in the world. By expanding our hearts, he can use us to heal and to teach others that the first lesson to learn is the centrality of their love relation with God—a relationship deep enough to draw them near to him even if they, like the Prodigal Son, are tempted to turn away. What could be a more fulfilling ministry than to realize that through us others can reach out and find God? Despite how low they are feeling, they may suddenly sense the tranquillity of his peace.

In this relation between meditation and ministry, Jesus is our best model. He goes off alone to ponder the will of the Father for his life. He knows his words will reach different ears with varying degrees of understanding and intensity. He resists at every turn the tendency to teach only a knowledgeable few, and hence he devises stories full of wisdom for all who would listen with docile hearts.

Moving down from the mountaintop of meditation, he enters the lively marketplace, where one beholds every imaginable form of human poverty. Meditation enriches his ministry, as it does ours. He knows what to say, what to do, which parable to tell, what advice to give.

Meditation prevents our ministry from degenerating into mere activism that exhausts us and in the end becomes offensive to others. If we are fostering meditation on a regular basis, its fruits cannot help but extend to our families, friends, places of work, and parishes. This practice encourages us to face life's ultimate meaning rather than to fall into dull routine, burying ourselves in sheer functionalism or losing our self-respect via wanton gratification. Without meditation on life's value, we might fall into a fog of addiction bearing little, if any, semblance to human responsibility.

As we calm down, ponder formative texts, and embody the experiences they record, we dip below the surface of life and gain access to its real meaning. We are not alone in our need for inner renewal, in our conviction that there is more to life than a useless cycle of birth, suffering, and death. This inner journey out of despair is motivated by our desire for union with God.

It is easier to make the journey from chaos to creativity when we listen to the assurance offered by the spiritual masters. The Lord never deserts us. He walks with us along the way. True, meditative reflection exposes us to the risk of having to alter our course. We can no longer rest content in the tangled forest of sin and duplicity. We must be willing to abdicate the egocentric throne and embrace the poverty of the cross.

We cannot cling to worn-out directives aimed at willful self-actualization if we want to listen to, reflect upon, and put into action these themes of Christian formation. One further aid in this process of renewal is that of keeping a spiritual notebook or journal, to which we shall devote the next chapter.[7]

---

7. See Richard J. Hauser, "Keeping a Spiritual Journal: Personal Reflections," *Review for Religious*, July–August 1983, pp. 575–84, for a description of how the practice of recording in a journal evolves, what method to follow, and what use one can make of the recordings.

7

Keeping a Journal

. . . whatever we are like in the words of our letters when we are absent, that is what we shall be like in our actions when we are present. (2 Co. 10:11)

I have always enjoyed reading the letters, diaries, and journals that enrich our collections of spiritual literature. Favorites of mine include, among others, Augustine's *Confessions;* Teresa of Avila's *The Book of Her Life;* Therese of Lisieux's *Story of a Soul;* Henry David Thoreau's *Walden;* Anne Frank's *The Diary of a Young Girl;* Dag Hammarskjöld's *Markings.*[1] The beauty, the integrity, the insight displayed in these texts awakens my admiration. I've read some of them again and again and have handed them on to others.

By the same token, in the face of such standards I used to fear keeping a journal of my own until I discovered in time and with much practice that journaling is one of the most helpful exercises we can do to increase our capacity for meditation and prayer. Pausing daily or a few times a week to jot

1. Complete references to these texts are found in the bibliography of this book.

down our thoughts has a way of quieting and uncluttering our overactive, decentered lives. Writing helps us to work through detected obstacles to spiritual living. Words allow our real concerns to well up, enabling us to find back our lost center in Christ. A journal is not only a record of events that touch and transform us; it is a private space in which we can meet ourselves in relation to others and God.

One could devise a litany of reasons to engage in journal writing, but to foster this practice it is first necessary to face some common objections to it. Let us deal with three typical reasons people give for not wanting to keep a journal. These reasons apply equally to a personal formation journal or to a notebook of reflections on spiritual reading dealing with resonances and resistances to the text.

The first objection people raise affects other spiritual practices too. It is "I don't have the time." Immediately this statement evokes the question "Do we manage time or does time manage us?" Is it true that time as such pressures us, or does the problem lie in our compulsion to check the clock?[2] How does it happen that tribal civilizations, lacking sophisticated devices by which to tell time, accomplish so much? How is it that people today, with ever-more refined instruments for measuring milliseconds, seconds, minutes, hours, and days, complain that they have no time to get anything done?

Time as such cannot pressure anyone; what pressures us is the way we interpret and measure time. If there is never enough, perhaps it is because we are trying to do too much at once and should really try to follow the directive posted on freeways: Slow down and live. What also strikes us as strange is that we somehow find the time to do the things we really want to do, like see a fine film, have lunch with a friend, play

2. See Edward Hall, *The Dance of Life: The Other Dimension of Time* (Garden City, N.Y.: Doubleday & Co., Inc., Anchor Books, 1983) for a brilliant analysis of time and its impact on people.

golf or tennis, spend a day shopping. What we don't have time for are the things we really don't feel like doing, and, notice, these often involve the more spiritual dimensions of our being. Hence, we don't have time to answer our correspondence, to do spiritual reading, to have the talk that's been pending for months with our teenager, to face up to the irritation building between us and our spouse. Not having time to keep a journal falls, of course, into the latter category.

While there is no easy solution to this problem of time versus us or us versus time, one way out of the dilemma is at least to begin examining what we do with our days and if the realm of spiritual living has any or a main priority. If it does, then we probably will find time for silence, formative reading, meditation, journaling, and prayer. We'll find the time for these expressions of spirituality because we want to, not because we have to or because someone is forcing us to do so. A life of transcendent meaningfulness becomes our top priority. Intimacy with God is the center around which we want the rest of our life to flow.

Some disciplining of the day may be necessary if we are to set aside periods for journaling. It's a matter of making a decision and gently persevering in that direction. Gentle is an important word here, lest we think that discipline means rigorous, militant compulsion. The opposite is true. Discipline is an outflow of discipleship. What could be more gentle than the relationship between a shepherding master like Christ and his band of followers? The only way to counter the objection that we don't have time for spiritual practices like journaling is simply to make sure that we do. Once we begin wisely allotting time for reading and reflection, wondering and writing, we shall soon notice the reward. Life becomes less pressured. Christ, not the clock on the wall, becomes the center of our lives. Amazingly, we seem to accomplish more because our energy is not siphoned into pockets of useless worry. What a joy it is to make time our servant instead of our becoming enslaved to time.

A second objection to journaling may involve our fear of confessional revelation. Some of us become paralyzed at the thought that someone may read what we've written. If we do write, the tendency is to edit our copy, just in case the diary is discovered! Besides the fact that the chances of this happening are slim to nonexistent, what difference does it make anyway when we're dead? If it makes that much difference, we can ask a friend to destroy the evidence once we're gone.

Let's look at the deeper reason behind this objection. It is not so much a blockage due to grandiose fantasies as it may be an unwillingness to share ourselves even with ourselves, let alone with others and God. It takes courage to share at this level of reflection. It is understandable that we fear digging below the surface to disclose the deeper meanings of life. It is tempting to substitute for reflective presence a superficial importance.

I know a person who always looks as if he's strutting toward the next appointment of earthshaking consequence. He never sits still long enough to share anything. He prides himself for living on the fly, managing ten or twenty projects at the same time, attending meetings he could skip or send a secretary to note. I cannot even imagine him engaging in a thoughtful, probing conversation. Every time I've been with him he has all the answers in advance. I find myself praying for him, wishing him well, but still wondering when the crash will occur. Surely one cannot live on such a high without paying the dual price of stress and inadequate human sharing. Does this poor soul, so overloaded with ideas and projects, have a true friend? Can he go on boasting of "hundreds of friends" without realizing that numbers cannot replace trusting human relations?

Journaling is a form of revelation, just as all writing is. It expresses something about ourself we may not even know. It is a form of discovery and disclosure, of drawing hidden thoughts and feelings out of prefocal vagueness into the clarity of focused consciousness. Journaling need not be an exercise in soul baring nor a violation of privacy. Understanding this right on the part of the journaler, to say some things and to leave others unsaid, dissolves the fear of *confessional* revelation while allowing for genuine self-disclosure. Sharing some things with ourselves on paper and retaining others in the silence of our heart is a privilege all journal writers exercise, be they as famous as Anne Morrow Lindbergh or as unknown as the lady next door. What we share with ourselves in a journal may or may not be shared with another.

The journal is really, to paraphrase Hammarskjöld, a nego-tiation between myself and God.[3] Keeping God's love and for-giveness uppermost in mind prevents this exercise from be-coming merely self-analytical. Journal writers know that they must guard against excessive introspection, that is to say, look-ing at themselves under a microscope, trying to analyze every fault and failing, every small success or consolation.

According to Adrian van Kaam, this anxiety-ridden, tense, guilty mode of introspection must give way to gentle, relaxed, forgiving, transcendent self-presence.[4] In journaling, I try to see myself and the daily ups and downs of life against the horizon of God's grand design for my formation. Self-judg-ment and negative imaging (what I'm not and can never be) give way in his loving presence to self-forgiveness and positive opportunity (what with his help I can at least try to do).

What counts, to use another phrase of van Kaam's,[5] are not dramatic shifts of personality but "just-noticeable-improve-

3. Dag Hammarskjöld, *Markings*, trans. Leif Sjoberg and W. H. Auden (London: Faber & Faber Inc., 1964), p. 7.
4. Adrian van Kaam, *In Search of Spiritual Identity* (Denville, N.J.: Dimension Books, 1975), pp. 172–96.
5. Adrian van Kaam, *Spirituality and the Gentle Life* (Denville, N.J.: Dimension Books, 1974), p. 122.

ments." I notice that I'm becoming a little more hospitable to others, ever so noticeably lighthearted, just enough of a more patient listener. Writing out what happens in dialogue with the Lord lessens this obstacle of unwillingness to share what I am going through. Journaling, like a conversation with a trusted friend or spiritual director, can be a first step toward bringing into the light the hindrances that block the path to harmonious human and Christian living.

A third objection to journaling falls into the category of if-I-can't-do-it-perfectly, I-don't-want-to-do-it-at-all. Underneath the familiar tactics of procrastination lurks the spectre of perfectionism. Perfectionism often poses under the guise of living up to religious ideals, but it really paralyzes some of us. It removes us from the imperfect human condition and raises impossible expectations about what we should or ought to be. We cannot bear to see our ordinary, ambivalent self displayed in everyday language on paper. We cannot stand the thought of later having to read what we've written. It all sounds so pedestrian, so drained of inspiration, so stupid and mundane. If we can't write something deeply meaningful and edifying, why write at all?

Related to this objection is the desire that the journal, each page and paragraph of it, be a finished product. One obstacle to honest journaling, to be avoided as much as possible, is the tendency to edit our copy. A journal is not a manuscript being readied for publication. It is a record of dialogue between ourself and God, a quiet reflection on a particular event to discover its formative or deformative meaning. While there is nothing wrong with trying to write out as clearly as possible what we mean, it might paralyze us if we try to foresee every possible misinterpretation of a future publisher or reader and try to respond to it. Again, we fail to see the importance of living in reality and writing things spontaneously as they come in response to a text, a conversation, a walk in nature, or whatever else of significance happens to us that we want to remember.

If we try too hard to solve our problems or to look simply great, the journal will soon become an impossible chore. It gets cast in the bottom bureau drawer, never to be seen or heard of again. It is only when we allow ourselves to make mistakes and explore their meaning that we can keep alive our interest in journaling. Perfectionism stops the flow of words faster than anything. Often the only way we can find the right path is to go around in circles for a while. We sometimes have to write many words before we can find the right combination to say what we mean. But what is creativity if not an ordering of chaos?

As the journal pages start to fill up, as we begin to read them over, we may find a few lights clicking on. We are able to make more connections between our daily life and the divine will. It may feel as if we are circling aimlessly around a certain point, when all of a sudden a pattern may emerge. We sense that we are on the right path, that our life is moving in the direction God wants us to go. Of course, we'll lose the way again, but for now the journal evidences that we've come to a moment of peace and rest. We may find ourselves writing something like these remarkable words of John Cardinal Newman, entitled *My Life's Work,* a text printed as a pamphlet I found on the pew of a Church.

> God has created me to do Him some definite service; He has committed some work to me which He has not committed to another. I have my mission—I may never know it in this life, but I shall be told it in the next . . . I shall do good, I shall do His work . . . if I do but keep His commandments and serve Him in my calling.
>
> Therefore I will trust Him whatever, wherever I am, I can never be thrown away. If I am in sickness, my sickness may serve Him; in perplexity, my perplexity may serve Him; if I am

in sorrow, my sorrow may serve Him. My sickness, or perplexity, or sorrow may be necessary causes of some great end, which is quite beyond us. He does nothing in vain. He may prolong my life, He may shorten it; He knows what He is about. He may take away my friends; He may throw me among strangers; He may make me feel desolate, make my spirit sink, hide the future from me. Still He knows what He is about.

O my God, I will put myself without reserve into Thy hands. Wealth or woe, joy or sorrow, friends or bereavement, honour or humiliation, good report or ill report, comfort or discomfort; Thy presence or Thy hiding of Thy countenance, all is good if it comes from Thee.

Thou art wisdom and Thou art love—what can I desire more? Thou hast led me in Thy counsel, and with glory Thou hast received me. What have I in heaven! And apart from Thee, what want I upon the earth? My flesh and my heart faileth; but God is the God of my heart and my portion forever.

Inspired by these words, how can we begin to counter our objections to journal writing? If we want to include this exercise as part of our spiritual practices, we might want to begin by writing letters to ourselves or reading the collected letters or journals left by others. In this way we can begin to develop some of the basic attitudes necessary for journaling: sensitivity to life situations, honesty, openness to divine directives. Letter writing and journal reading become incentives for further expressing our thoughts on paper. In this way we become more aware, awake, and attentive to the many opportunities daily life offers for spiritual growth.

Once we decide to start, are there any concrete aids to journal writing a practitioner may suggest? What incentives can we find to keep going? It is first of all fascinating to realize that the act of writing fixates on paper the stream of experience constantly slipping away from us. It helps us to remember a few important events among the mass of happenings we experience. Writing stops the flow of experience so that we can look at it again and gain insight into what was really occurring in this meeting or in the presence of such a text or during our pause for prayer and presence to the transcendent. Journaling in this regard could be compared to the construction of a dam on a river. The dam stops the rush of water for the sake of rechanneling it for higher yields of power. Similarly, writing channels our attention so that we can see more clearly the mystery of God's directing will in daily events.

Journaling opens us to the possibility of enjoying an interior adventure or, to use the words of Loren Eiseley, of exploring the "ghost continent" within us.[6] Facing our true limits and talents encourages us not to try to be anyone but the person we are. This inner venture becomes more exciting as the frontiers of exterior experience become smaller and smaller. Growing older means doing less in terms of quantity, not quality.

Tracing these passages from one phase of life to the next can teach us much about our transcendent possibilities.[7] We all know people who, though weakened vitally and slowed down functionally, are gentle, gracious souls, full of the wisdom of life. I am in correspondence with a few such persons. One of them is an older religious woman, whose letters sound like entries from a spiritual journal. She seems to live by St. Paul's words: ". . . though this outer man of ours may be falling into decay, the inner man is renewed day by day" (2 Co. 4:16). On the occasion of her seventy-fifth birthday, she wrote the following letter to me.

Do you think it's unusual that I keep discovering hidden teachers in my life? I'm convinced one is never too old to learn.

6. Loren Eiseley, *The Unexpected Universe* (Middlesex, England: Penguin Books Inc., 1973), pp. 13–29.
7. Reflection on these passages and phases of development through mid-life and aging can be found in Daniel J. Levinson, *The Seasons of a Man's Life* (New York: Alfred A. Knopf Inc., 1978) and Adrian van Kaam, *The Transcendent Self* (Denville, N.J.: Dimension Books, 1979).

For example, yesterday, when I made that early morning walk around the garden of the monastery, amidst my beloved olive trees, I saw the most glorious spider web glistening with dew. The spider rested at its center, oblivious of my admiration for its nightly work. I thought of God's work as the continual creation of these intricate webs, with us at the center of his spinning. The older I grow, the more I seem to behold the spiritual richness of daily reality. I'm more conscious than ever before of things in their remarkable particularity, as our Zen friends say. I see oranges as oranges, chapel pews as pews, spoons as spoons—and it is all wonderful, marvelous. How can I explain this emergent awe before the simplest things? A few years ago, I would have overlooked all of them, not now. Now I want to hold these incidents of "god-seeing," as I call them, close to my heart, just as one treasures a worn photo. I know you'll understand what I mean.

Truly I know what she is saying, and I find in her words a real incentive for journal-keeping. Recording these apparently innocent events makes us aware of the timeless mystery permeating every particle of creation. Engaging in the discipline of listening-seeing-writing does awaken us to the hidden teachers everywhere. Our interiority is immensely enriched by this exercise. I could not possibly imagine my friend being bored, for her life is full of fresh discoveries. Though her range of outer activity is increasingly curtailed, her inner life is more rich than ever. New intuitions, feelings, insights fill her letters. She has become for me and for many others a living spiritual teacher. By keeping track in her journal of what life discloses to her, she is able to live each day to the full. She can then record for herself and others what she has learned from life from having lived it.

Another incentive for journal-keeping has to do with developing our formative as distinct from our functional memory. The latter refers to rote memory, to the facts and figures we need to function well in society and our profession. The former refers to lived memory, that remembrance of the past that lives on in the present and future. Journaling enables us to keep track of those persons and events that really mean something to us. It enables us to lift out of life's flow those moments that have a forming effect, for better or worse, on our lives.

The journal is not only a place to record good memories; it is also the locus for working through bad experiences and bringing ourselves to the point of healing forgiveness. In regard to the past, a journal can also temper our nostalgic romanticizing about the "good old days," which probably never existed in quite the way we recall. Remembering in the golden glow of nostalgia is one thing; reading an actual record of what happened is another. Thus a journal, kept regularly over a number of years, can provide us with a realistic perspective on our life's journey. We can sense its real design, pattern, network—not our fantasy about what might have happened, but our real memory of what did.

Knowing that life patterns can emerge is another incentive to journal-keeping. Too often we are inclined to believe that our life is chaotic, a series of incidental events without rhyme or reason. The journal shows us that this is not the case. In fact, many fine things have happened to us. Our life has been meaningful to many people. What happens here is similar to looking through the photograph album. We may be inclined to think that nothing much happened, that life passed us by, but the photos belie this conclusion. We did go places and do things; we made friends and kept them; we were important to our parents; we saw our children through school and enjoyed family celebrations.

Rereading old journals convinces us that our life was not haphazard. It has a purpose in God's eyes and our own. Think of all those times our faith carried us through. It was awfully hard to see why things happened the way they did then, but now we understand the reason. God knew what he was doing, even during times of suffering or family tragedy. Despite these limits and imperfections, there is a meaning to life we would not trade for anything. Thus our journal becomes a source of hope, a confirmation of our place in God's forming plan. It reveals the mystery that out of so much that is flawed there can emerge something truly fine.

As a last incentive, it is good to know that a journal can be a tremendous safety valve. By this I mean that it can be a safe, private place in which to vent some of our anger, confusion, pain. Writing releases pent-up, potentially volcanic emotions. I can let go of a lot that disturbs me when I begin to write. Immense mountains are relativized into normal molehills, once I see them sketched on paper. If I don't write out these hurts and angers, they have a way of festering inside, of tormenting me until the time comes when I inappropriately explode. Composition spends rage. It humanizes the situation, evokes compassion, puts this incident against the horizon of the infinite. Expression of emotion leaves more space in my heart for silence, appraisal, prayer. Less energy is spent being angry, more is available for forgiveness.

The opposite is also true. Little or no composition dims my powers of reflection. I'm more inclined to act and react impulsively. I lose the art of blending reason and feeling in response to any situation, be it painful or joyful. Lacking expression, my life may remain rather thoughtless and superficial. I go through the motions of living, but my life inside is like a blank page. I pick up ideas of others and react to them but never have any thoughts of my own.

If I consistently refuse to take time for reflection, I run the risk of a dull, uninspiring existence, a kind of death in life. Just gaze at the faces of people waiting in lines for subways and buses. Their zombielike glaze can be depressing. One look and we ask ourselves, "Is that all? Is there no more to life than this living death?" The fierce resistance of such a posture is found in the diaries of a person like Anne Morrow Lindbergh, who declared, "We must be open to all points of the compass; husband, children, friends, home, community; stretched out, exposed, sensitive like a spider's web to each breeze that blows, to each call that comes."[8] This awareness, this wakeful attention, is an essential condition for the spiritual life.

Having presented these incentives for journal-keeping, let us ask in summary what kinds of things a journal can contain. Then we shall suggest a few concrete guidelines regarding how a journal can be kept. From all that we have said, it is clear that a journal can be a running log of daily experiences, or a record of significant events, or both. In this way we become sensitive to the myriad details of life, to the richness of the ordinary, to the sacrament of the present moment.

Formative events selected out of the wider stream of life are like stepping-stones in the midst of a pond. Recording them helps us to get in touch with the patterns of our life as a whole, with those key situations that constitute our place in God's plan. Looking back on these entries, we may see the threads of our experience tying together and forming a meaningful mosaic. This influential person, that significant period of transition—all make more sense when we see the whole tapestry.

Recall Augustine's *Confessions* in this light. His meeting with St. Ambrose and his encounter with the scripture text read in the garden, following a long period of doubt and debate with God, were threads that suddenly came together. He saw, as if for the first time, the meaning of his life in relation to the Church. He beheld the guiding hand of God in the events leading up to his conversion, when he was able at last to let that hand lead him in all that was to follow.[9]

8. Anne Morrow Lindbergh, *Gift from the Sea* (New York: Random House Inc., Vintage Trade Books, 1965), p. 28.
9. *The Confessions of St. Augustine,* trans. John K. Ryan (Garden City, N.Y.: Doubleday & Co., Inc., Image Books, 1960), book 8, chapter 12, pp. 201–03.

In addition to this linear movement, a journal can also be an occasion for spiraling down and reflecting on a significant personal experience, the ramifications of which cannot be grasped in one writing. A moment that impacts upon us can evoke several spiral reflections over a number of years. Such moments usually touch the core of who we are and compel us to catch ourselves before we betray our congeniality, the deepest core of who we are before God. An obvious example would be the point in time at which we are faced with choosing a profession. Parents, teachers, peers may be pulling us in one direction, but we feel increasingly unhappy with their choice for us. We need to ask, "Who am I? What am I called to be in dialogue with my limits and possibilities? What can I do in this given situation, with these people who depend on me or look to me for guidance? Where can I find the courage to listen to the still, small voice inside that beckons me in a direction others may not understand?"

Such crossroad moments of life may merit several journal entries. As Anne Frank wrote in her diary, ". . . paper is more patient than man."[10] It is a lot more patient than other people, who with the best of intentions may pressure us to be someone who we are not. Paper can be a true friend at such times, as Anne's diary, nicknamed "Kitty," was a friend to her. Kitty understood the real Anne underneath the raucous teenager. Generations of readers can thank Kitty for being so patient with Anne, for helping her to be honest with herself and to find the voice inside that was her own. That voice is in all of us, and our journal may help us to let it speak. This is the voice of our uniqueness, and it alone can ultimately be shared with others.

With these two movements, linear and spiral, in mind, what practical advice can we disclose for the keeping of a journal?

10. Anne Frank, *The Diary of a Young Girl,* trans. B. M. Mooyaart-Doubleday (New York: Modern Library, Inc., 1952), p. 12.

First of all, we have to build time for journaling into our daily or weekly schedule. Like any spiritual practice, this too requires a certain regularity. Secondly, it is good to pause for a few moments before we actually begin to write to collect our thoughts and to decide what the general focus of our entry will be. Linear or spiral? Recopying a text that appeals to us or reflecting on its meaning? It is hard to predict in what direction writing will take us because there is a kind of self-generating power to written words. One phrase, one sentence, one paragraph may lead to another. Our pen may flow over the page, or we may struggle for each word. How rested or how pressured we feel has an effect here.

If we feel incapable of writing, then it is best not to force ourselves too much. It's good to try to pen something because at times when we feel most depleted, simply beginning to write stimulates us, so much so that we may surprise ourselves with a finished page. It may also happen that what we write moves from description-reflection into dialogue with God. Our journal entry becomes like a letter to him. If our pen slows to a standstill, that may be a signal to pick up our text and begin reading for a while. Suddenly a text will spark a thought and we can turn to our journal and write out what we are feeling. While it is not advisable to force ourselves to write, neither is it wise to wait for an inspiration that may never come. Some discipline is necessary here, but within it we can find our own rhythms.

The question may arise, Is journal-keeping for everyone? I would have to answer honestly no. This practice is not foundational in that sense. We encourage it, we believe in its efficacy for spiritual living, but experience shows that some people do not, cannot, write journals on a regular basis. It may be enough for them to read the diaries and journals of kindred souls without feeling that they have to face a blank page of their own.

Should journal-keeping be a good practice for us, we can see from other journals that writers who use this genre for spiritual deepening tend to be specific, descriptive, and concrete. Good examples would be John Cardinal Newman's *Apologia pro Vita Sua;* Pope John XXIII's *Journal of a Soul;* Anne Morrow Lindbergh's *Bring Me a Unicorn;* Annie Dillard's *Pilgrim at Tinker Creek.* These authors deal in particulars of daily life, not in abstractions pertinent to "all people." Journal writers report details that matter for the whole of their lives, not fleeting emotions. They seek patterns of meaning in the briefest encounters. The act of writing enables them to haul to the surface thoughts they did not know were there. It shapes the blur of ideas, notions, and hunches, leading to knowledge of self, others, and God. Journaling keeps us from spinning half-truths and pulling one point out of the whole perspective of life. By keeping a journal we have an opportunity to go back to this or that insight and reflect on it again. Each reflection helps us to personalize even more what we have learned about our formation journey.

A journal honestly kept reveals that in the most ordinary of lives, we are not alone. Others have traversed the same terrain. The journal also provides an opportunity for growth in gratitude and humility. We feel grateful that the Lord has graced us with new insights into things that keep us from being more closely united to him. We feel humbled at the thought of his love and care in granting us these graces. Had we not kept a journal, these sentiments would not have been aroused, for the original thoughts this writing generated would simply not have been available to us.

Such writing serves as a means of integration. It enables us to slow down and gather together otherwise scattered thoughts and feelings. We can better understand what dispositions we need to foster at this moment to live a more Christ-centered life and what obstacles stand in the way of this integration.

Writing reveals pitfalls on the road to consonant living and detours we might best avoid. It fosters the right balance between acknowledged limits and fresh opportunities for spiritual liberation. Above all, writing helps us to harness floating insights and impressions in concrete words. Once these are fixated on a page, they bear testimony to our good intentions and efforts to grow more like the Lord day by day. Silently, reflectively, prayerfully, without isolated introspection, force, or manipulation, we wait upon the Lord in these words. We wait until he allows us to touch the living stream, the source from which all words spring.

Thus, journal writing, which seems such a singular experience, becomes an entrance into the universal quest for spiritual meaning. It fosters a playful, hope-filled approach to living. Far from being a harsh discipline, journal-keeping becomes a condition for the possibility of free, creative self-expression, bringing us into communion with the Personhood of God. It makes explicit the ways he has been working in our life. We feel the power and gentleness of the Lord in the gifted nature of these events. The written word evokes our consent to his plan, a yes freely given because journaling helps us to see more clearly how straight he writes in the crooked lines of life.

In working through our initial resistance, we find ourselves led to increasing resonance with his will, to an attitude of genuine surrender released from the bonds of ego control. To write down these negotiations between us and God involves risk, trust, humility, integrity, and faith. We realize that only to the degree that we are nourished and transformed by his word can we grow in the art of graciously serving others in his name. Since this art is wholly dependent on the life of prayer, it is to prayer that our attention must turn next.

8

Becoming
a Prayerful Presence

. . . my house will be a house of prayer . . . (Lk. 19:46)

"House" as a symbol has many levels of meaning. A Cape Cod village is recognizable by houses covered with weather-beaten shingles. The body has been called the house of the spirit. Supermarkets house groceries, meats, and vegetables necessary for survival. God calls his house the universe, and the Church a house of prayer. Prayer is, therefore, the most encompassing experience of the spiritual life. It is as essential to the spirit's unfolding as bread is to the body.

Spiritual masters are fond of saying that if we know how to breathe, we know how to pray, for breath is as natural to the body's function as prayer is to the spirit. The universe itself inhales and exhales the spirit of God. Humankind is no different. We too live in God's house, and his house is a house of prayer.

People still wonder how to pray and how they can simultaneously live a life of prayer and be of service to the world. Though worship and work are meant to be coordinated, we are inclined to see them as separate entities because we have made prayer into a complicated exercise, fine for contemplatives but not easy for people in the world. We have forgotten that prayer is as natural to us as breath. Thus we have to remind ourselves in this chapter that prayer is not remote from life but integral to it. Let's call to mind a few examples.

Have you ever sat in a doctor's office awaiting the outcome of tests for a serious condition? You have probably called upon God for strength and asked him to take away this cross, if it be his will.

Have you ever approached a funeral parlor, knowing that the persons inside are going to ask you why this death occurred so senselessly, so soon, since their son or daughter was the victim of a drunken driver? You beg God to help you find words of consolation that are not textbook replies.

Have you beheld a child take its first steps and spontaneously prayed that God would protect this little one from too much pain?

These are but a few instances of how much a part of life prayer is. God's name is on our lips in major and minor cases. Our need for his blessing does not cease. We turn to him when we seek the meaning of an upsetting event, when we feel uninspired and depleted of energy, when we lack the strength to do a job well. Likewise, we feel his nearness during the liturgy, while talking to a trusted friend, in the midst of a family celebration. People tell us they pray best when in their garden, while rocking in a favorite chair, or walking by the shore. No experience, however rough or smooth, has to exclude God. He is potentially present in all we say and do. Paradoxically, he is often most near to us when he seems to be farthest away.

Prayer is this continual interaction between us and God. It is the room in our hearts where God dwells always, the inner house his spirit fills. At times we are explicitly present to him in a posture of worship; at other times we are too busy to do anything but implicitly recall his promise.

Prayer is like a reservoir of divine energy continually being refilled inside us so that we can share its power with others in the world. If this is true, then how do we move from merely saying prayers, to ourselves becoming living prayer?[1] The answer may be clear if we look at Jesus' encounter with the Samaritan woman (Jn. 4:4–42).[2] He takes this woman, deformed as she is by egocentric desires, and draws her forth to worship the Father in spirit and truth. In the course of their encounter, he leads her from doubt, to petitionary prayer, to pure adoration.

We learn from this story that prayer means being able to converse familiarly with God at all times. It is not only a matter of asking for what we need but of living always in an attitude of thankfulness. Because God holds us in being, we can behold him in prayer. We can walk with him, hand in hand, detached enough from selfish desires to sense his spirit everywhere. We see, as it were, the invisible order of reality behind the visible. Like the Samaritan woman, we are astonished by the truth that God has come down from the mountaintop into the marketplace to seek us, to forgive us, to embrace us.

Prayer understood in this light is not a complicated procedure. It is as simple as breathing, as wondering, as beholding the mystery that lovingly holds us. We can no more stand outside this all-embracing love than a starfish can exist outside the sea. Sadly, however, we can erect obstacles to our becoming a prayerful presence. For instance, if we think of prayer as

1. See Anthony Bloom, *Living Prayer* (Springfield, Ill.: Templegate Publishers, 1966), especially pp. 9–19 on "The Essence of Prayer."
2. See also Adrian van Kaam, *Woman at the Well* (Denville, N.J.: Dimension Books, 1976).

a magic formula for conjuring up our desires and fulfilling them, we may give up trying when our wishes are not granted. We are like little children who only maintain interest in a game when they are winning. We have tragically narrowed the mystery of God's allowing will by reducing it to the parameters of our understanding.

We can also become so preoccupied with our careers that we feel indifferent toward the Transcendent. Our success enriches us with worldly acclaim but impoverishes us spiritually. Worship is crushed under the weight of accomplishment. Doing excludes being in quiet presence before God. Self-sufficiency carried to this extreme tragically severs one from a sense of the Sacred. We no longer resonate with the abiding presence of God. The bond of intimacy between us and him is broken by our forgetfulness. Our hope resides in the fact that though we may resist or refuse his presence, his gift of prayer, it is there for the asking if we but open the door.

Living in a prayerful attitude implies both awareness of and assent to the divine direction of our lives. Being open to God's loving and allowing will is not a matter of quietistic indifference but of receptive dialogue. We try to see each event as a challenge, as a point of departure for discovering, despite our feeling of ambiguity, what God wants us to do and be.

His will is not written in black and white. He appeals to us through our concrete situation. Our appraisal of what he asks has to take into account our past history, our present commitments, our future goals. The directives we receive in this way, once appraised, impel us with God's help to give new form and meaning to our unique and communal situation. In prayerful attentiveness, though we may not always understand what is happening to us, we may at least begin to accept the events of our life, be they painful or joyful, be they occasions of near despair or newfound hope, as part of his divine plan.

Becoming prayerful persons means attuning ourselves to the

symphony of formation enfolding and energizing us at all times. We meet God in a sunrise, a smiling face, an inspiring text. We detect in unexpected quarters, like a hospital bed, his providential care. We realize that the dross of human fallibility covers the gold of human dignity. That is why we sense his presence in an aging parent, a sick child, a crippled beggar—in all who are suffering, vulnerable, imperfect.

All persons, events, and things begin to speak to us of God. He appears in the strangest places and never ceases to surprise us. Who could have thought, for that matter, that the Word would become flesh in an obscure spot like Bethlehem or that redemption would come to us on a cross?

I remember in this regard the day I was washing lettuce with the sun shining through the kitchen window. Suddenly I felt inclined to hold one of the leaves up to the light to see more clearly its delicately veined structure. Before I knew what was happening, I was drawn into deep prayer. How wonderful, how awesome, O God, is your epiphany in creation.

Something similar occurred when I held the hand of my baby nephew. Dear Lord, how could anything be wrought so finely as this finger?

Prayer wells up at these unexpected moments if we flow with their invitation. What is around and within us, the most ordinary appearances, become openings to God for the prayerful person.[3] Life is, after all, made up of a series of moments strung along the thin thread we call our destiny or direction. We live these moments from day to day, seldom taking much notice of them. They are part of the taken-for-granted. We awake, rise, dress, drive to work. There is nothing noticeable in that; it is just the start of another working day. We may go along like this for a long time. Then something breaks in. Time

3. See also Charles Cummings, *The Mystery of the Ordinary* (San Francisco: Harper & Row Publishers, Inc., 1982).

comes to a standstill, and we begin to think, to pray. The pattern of our life comes into relief.

What is this "something"? Sudden suffering. A death in the family. The betrayal of trust. A frown on our supervisor's face. The discovery that the grocer overcharged us. A national disaster. The crash of a plane I could have been on. Lack of courtesy from a parking lot attendant. Symbolic pointers like these signify our vulnerability, our need for compassion. They can be, and often are, occasions of prayer, as we say to God, "Why?" or "Please," or "Help."

Once in a journal entry I sketched out the scenario of what becoming a prayerful presence might mean.

> Morning dawns. I awaken slowly and take an extra moment to say thanks for the gift of this day. I eat and feel grateful for the food on my table. While dressing, I try to center my thoughts on the Lord. "Even if I do not think of You explicitly, let me do what I do for Your sake." While watching my driving, I can still take a few moments for recollection. I stop at the traffic light and look out over hills, knowing that His presence is everywhere. I intersperse mental plans for my morning with brief meditations on His providential care. In this way I save myself a lot of needless aggravation over a day that will work itself out anyway. By the time I arrive at the office, my working day has already taken on a deeper meaning. What might have been a merely functional approach is replaced by a rhythmic blend of action and contemplation, labor and leisure—and all because of a shift in attitude. Whether preparing reports or chairing meetings, my whole approach will be more calm and peaceful, if my time is grounded in the eternal. I realize that I can be patient. Life is a gradual unfolding. What I do not accomplish today, I can do tomorrow. My time becomes more God's time. In his good time, all tensions are resolved.[4]

4. Susan Annette Muto, *Approaching the Sacred: An Introduction to Spiritual Reading* (Denville, N.J.: Dimension Books, 1973), pp. 104–05.

We pray alone, of course, but we also pray as members of a community of faith, of a Church with a rich heritage and tradition. Our small prayers are inserted into the great stream of the Judeo-Christian liturgy, psalms, and devotions. These common prayers complement our personal petitions and raise worship above subjective expression. In the hymnal, for example, we find a gamut of expressions and emotions summarizing how God's people cry out for help, give glory to his name, plea for Christian unity, celebrate his birth, crucifixion, and resurrection from the dead. We can also research forms of prayer and meditation that have led people of other faiths to foster presence to the Holy.[5]

Prayer as a way of being expresses itself in many ways. It can be a cry arising from anguish and torment, from loneliness and desolation; a song of joy ringing out in a moment of jubilation; a wordless peace between friends; a plea or intercession; a silent exchange between lover and Beloved.

Prayer is many things, yet it is one. It is the soaring of the human spirit to meet and be with the Spirit of God. It is heart calling to Heart, the alone with the Alone, the finite before the Infinite, the temporal at home with the Eternal. In prayer our human misery finds solace and strength in God's mercy.

What gauges the depth or superficiality of this bonding is its fruit in daily life. One person goes to Church, utters liturgical prayers in a perfunctory way, and goes about his or her business. Another prays these words fervently, letting their meaning touch and stir the heart to imitate Christ's attitudes and actions throughout the week. Such persons join with the Lord to form a community whose bond is prayer.

We become living prayer when prayer affects every act and decision of our life. The world for us is not a place where

5. For an exhaustive, convincing treatment of the place of meditation in the life of prayer, see Patricia Carrington, *Freedom in Meditation* (Garden City, N.Y.: Doubleday & Co., Inc., Anchor Books, 1978).

people fight for survival but a house of prayer. Praying is not an experience reserved for a holy elite, but a mode of physical, functional, and spiritual survival. The choice is ours: we can erect barriers between ourselves and God, close doors, mete out love in stingy dribbles, and reap the meager results; or we can love God with our whole heart, soul, mind, and strength, pray without ceasing, and become the fully alive people he wants us to be.

Jacopone da Todi, a spiritual master of the thirteenth century in the Franciscan tradition, raised prayer to the level of ecstatic poetry. Like all spiritual seekers, Jacopone descended into the depths of his soul and struggled over a lifetime to respond fully to God's love. In a world inclined to give other relations and responsibilities primacy, Jacopone found, as did St. Francis of Assisi and St. John of the Cross, that in repentance, poverty, and prayer one finds God as one's true center. This relation alone sends the heart soaring in jubilation, as Jacopone's words express in this poem, *Laud 76.*

> *O heart's jubilation, love and song,*
> *Joy and joy unceasing,*
> *The stuttering of the unutterable—*
> *How can the heart but sing?*
>
> *Joy shooting upward uncontrollably,*
> *Where is the heart to contain it?*
> *O shouting and singing oblivious of all,*
> *Joy brimmed to overflowing!*
>
> *O jubilant joy and somersaults of happiness,*
> *Pray, learn to be prudent:*
> *Sensible people with sensible smiles*
> *Cannot understand the wildness of your ecstasy!*
>
> *Learn to conceal the bliss*
> *Throbbing thickly beneath the surface;*

There is meaning all unknown to sensible people
In the joyous gyrations of the wounded heart.[6]

Prayer in the end is about this all consuming love relation between God and us. It is a conscious realization of the union that is already effected between our souls and God by grace. The immediate end of prayer may be to consider some mystery of Christ's life, to resolve a problem, to seek guidance for a practical course of action. But the ultimate end of prayer is always communion with God. It is receptivity to his self-communication in silence and in the course of life situations. It is continually discovering God at the center of our being so that we can carry him into the midst of our doing.

We realize that we can reach out to God only because he has already drawn us to himself. Our love for him, no matter how intense, is but a dim reflection of his prior and sustaining love for us. The prayer we pray is not our own doing but the voice of the Spirit who pleads for us in sighs and longings that words cannot express (Rm. 8:26–27).

The more we listen in attentive silence, the more we wait upon the Word in faithful expectancy, the more we approach contemplation—a gift attained not by strenuous effort or intellectual exercise, but out of the pure abundance of God's love. Listen again to Jacopone at prayer in *Laud* 90.

Let no man mock me, then,
If that Love drives me to madness.
Once captured, no heart can shield itself,
Or escape Love's hold.
How can it withstand the searing flame
Without turning to ashes?
Where can I find someone who can understand,
Who can take pity on me in my agony?

6. Jacopone da Todi, *The Lauds,* trans. Serge and Elizabeth Hughes, in *The Classics of Western Spirituality* (New York: Paulist Press, 1982), pp. 227–28.

For heaven and earth and all things created
Cry out insistently that I should love:
"Make haste to embrace the Love
That made us all, love with all your heart!
Because that Love so desires you
He uses all things to draw you to Himself."
I see all goodness and beauty and gentleness
Spilling out of this superabundance of holy light!

Oh, that my heart would not stumble and sag!
That I were able to love more intensely,
That I had more than myself to give
To that measureless light,
That sweet splendor.
I have given all that I have
To possess the Lover who constantly renews me,
That ancient Beauty forever new!

At the sight of such beauty I am swept up
Out of myself to who knows where;
My heart melts, like wax near fire,
Christ puts His mark on me, and stripped of myself
(O wondrous exchange!) I put on Christ.
Robed in this precious garment,
Crying out its love,
The soul drowns in ecstasy![7]

7. Ibid., pp. 258–59.

9

Approaching Contemplation

As every structure is aligned on him, all grow into one holy temple in the Lord; and you too, in him, are being built into a house where God lives, in the Spirit. (Ep. 2:21–22)

Approaching contemplation means accepting the awesome fact that we are all growing into "one holy temple in the Lord." Despite our frailty and fears, we are being "built into a house where God lives." This temple, this house that we are, is founded on faith. We approach contemplation the moment we make an act of faith in the omnipotence and omnipresence of God.[1] To contemplate means to be in the temple of the Lord, sensing, believing, and experiencing that we are actually in his presence, that he is in us and we are in him. This basic union never changes, whatever obstacles we may place on the contemplative path. God is with us and for us, however lost and confused we may be.

1. For a comparison of Oriental and Christian approaches to God, see Yves Raguin, *Paths to Contemplation,* Religious Experience Series, vol. 6 (St. Meinrad, Ind.: Abbey Press, 1974).

If this bond between us and God is so deep, what can we do to live more contemplatively? What discipline is required of us if we are to be drawn ever more deeply into divine intimacy? We know that the very act of placing our foot on the path is due solely to God's grace. Cooperating with this grace means letting go of our prideful, rebellious, selfish tendencies in order to let his peace expand and penetrate our hearts and minds, our whole being.

Silence, spiritual reading, meditation, and prayer have led us already to value a life of worshipful presence to God in the world. We have come to know ourselves a little better in relation to his plan for our lives. Through stillness and listening, in reflection and prayerful receptivity, we have appraised and acted upon divine directives as these are disclosed in our daily situation. These spiritual disciplines, if faithfully practiced, prepare us to abide in contemplative presence in the holy temple of the Lord, who bestows upon us his gift of peace.[2]

Contemplatives are no different in essence from ordinary people. They strive to obey God's commandments, to flow with the teachings and traditions of the Church, to live up to their commitments, to work honestly and hard. But they do all of these things out of an inner motivation to temper their ego so thoroughly that it is no longer they who live, but Christ who lives in them (Ga. 2:20). His gift of peace frees them from the vicissitudes of consolation or desolation. Guided by grace, they become increasingly aware of his manifestations in creation, suffering with him in those who suffer, rejoicing with him in those who rejoice. One's whole life thus becomes an orientation to God.

How do we reach this new terrain of intimacy with God? Clearly he alone can draw us into the depths of contemplative

---

2. The connection between practice and contemplation is developed more fully by Ronald V. Wells, *Spiritual Disciplines for Everyday Living* (Schenectady, N.Y.: Character Research Press, 1982).

prayer and transformation in Christ. On our part, openness to his invitation is essential, despite the risk of renewal that is involved. The journey to union presupposes always a dying and a rising. It is a personal recurrence, spiritually speaking, of the Paschal Mystery. What has to die is not our deepest self, our being made in the form and likeness of God, but the illusion that our functional ego is all-powerful. Once we shed the imprisoning restrictions of self-centeredness, we acknowledge anew our sheer dependency on God. In faith, hope, and love, we are free to serve him with our whole heart and mind and to care for others as we would have them care for us. Letting go of unholy pride thus enables us to enjoy the holy nobility God has granted us as his most original gift.

The spiritual masters convince us that the ascetical life is the best basis to prepare for the gift of a sound mystical life, that is to say, "a house where God lives, in the Spirit." Despite a wide variety of directives regarding self-discipline, the masters of the spiritual life, be they desert dwellers or mystics in the city, would agree that we must give up our desires for things or relations that can never satisfy us fully so that we can attend to the one Good in whose presence we find and approximate the fullness of peace and joy, reached totally only in the life to come.

This is the basic meaning of asceticism: to break through the illusion that anyone or anything but God can fulfill our desire for holiness and happiness. Whatever comes close to doing so is but a pointer to what is beyond—not an end in itself but a means toward our goal. God alone can quench this thirst for beauty, goodness, and truth that entraps the human heart. Our souls, to paraphrase the famous text of St. Augustine, "are restless until they rest in God."

Asceticism also means acknowledging our utter dependence on God, which is to say, giving up any perfectionistic project of self-salvation. We can never redeem ourselves nor merit the saving graces God so liberally bestows. Obeying God's law is good and essential, but of itself it cannot save us. Without love our spiritual life is dead, even though we may boast of our moral uprightness.

The approach to contemplation thus involves the *slow relinquishing over a lifetime* of desires that stand between us and full surrender to God. We need to relativize whatever we have made ultimate besides him. As long as we cling to anything or anyone less than God, as if such were the entire truth and meaning of life, we can never experience the sheer joy of soaring freely, without hindrance, to our divine source. Such is the experience contemplatives seek.

Once we are more or less freed from excessive attachments, we are free for the next step which, simply put, involves waiting upon God in our inner and outer life. Inwardly speaking, our prayer becomes more detached and receptive, less demanding and discursive. We try to be with God in all circumstances without knowing exactly where he may be leading us. We let go of our expectations and wait upon his revelations.

Outwardly speaking, we try to let all that we say, see, and do become a pointer to God's eternal glory. Our talents are gifts he has given to lead others to behold his face in creation, humanity, and world. Our service to others is not a search for personal acclaim but a labor of love. As a result we begin to live in charity and humility, virtues which the masters agree are sure and essential companions of contemplation.

One other sign that we are on the way may come paradoxically in the form of dryness or aridity in our prayer life. The process by which God purifies our sensual and spiritual desires is bound at times to be painful. Yet the new lights he allows to glow in our soul can only be fully appreciated against the background of dark and dry self-stripping.

When we feel most forgotten and forsaken, like Jesus in Gethsemane, at that moment of supreme agony by human standards, we may be most intimately united with God. He leads us through this narrow way of the cross so that we can pass from death to self to new life in him.

We too have to strip off the garments of gratification as the Lord was stripped on Calvary. Thus naked, there is nothing left to cling to but faith, hope, and love. God can then transform this nothingness we feel into the living flame of his love.[3] We learn to trust aridity and absence as a positive sign of his deeper presence. We welcome divine purification whenever it comes, in whatever inner or outer form it takes. Our experience slowly convinces us that such suffering is but a prelude to illumination. St. John of the Cross's words affirm this paradox, telling us,

> . . . even though this happy night darkens the spirit, it does so only to impart light concerning all things; and even though it humbles a person and reveals his miseries, it does so only to exalt him; and even though it impoverishes and empties him of all possessions and natural affection, it does so only that he may reach out divinely to the enjoyment of all earthly and heavenly things, with a general freedom of spirit in them all.[4]

The style of prayer we feel drawn to at this stage is not discursive but still, not wordy but quiet, not image-ladened but either imageless or focused on one word, symbol, or text. According to St. John of the Cross, many persons make the mistake of disturbing their souls with concepts and conclusions when in reality an inner voice is beseeching them to abide in the calm and repose of interior quietude, which is filled with the peace and refreshment of the Holy Spirit. Therefore,

> when the spiritual person cannot meditate, he should learn to remain in God's presence with a loving attention and a tranquil

3. See *The Living Flame of Love* in *The Collected Works of St. John of the Cross,* trans. Kieran Kavanaugh, O.C.D. and Otilio Rodriguez, O.C.D. (Washington, D.C.: Institute of Carmelite Studies, ICS Publications, 1973), pp. 577–649.
4. *The Dark Night,* book 2, chap. 9, in *Collected Works of St. John,* p. 346.

intellect, even though he seems to himself to be idle. For little by little and very soon the divine calm and peace with a wondrous, sublime knowledge of God, enveloped in divine love, will be infused into his soul. He should not interfere with forms or discursive meditations and imaginings. Otherwise his soul will be disquieted and drawn out of its peaceful contentment to distaste and repugnance. And if, as we said, scruples about his inactivity arise, he should remember that pacification of soul (making it calm and peaceful, inactive and desireless) is no small accomplishment. This, indeed, is what our Lord asks of us through David: *Vacate et videte quoniam ego sum Deus* (Ps. 45:11). This would be like saying: Learn to be empty of all things—interiorly and exteriorly—and you will behold that I am God.[5]

At such moments cares and concerns fade into the background, and one feels drawn mysteriously toward God. The author of *The Cloud of Unknowing* suggests a simple method by which we can press all images, distractions, and memories of past sins and future expectations under the "cloud of forgetting" so that we can enter the "cloud of unknowing" with longing love.[6] He says that we are to lift our hearts up to God with a gentle stirring of love regardless of the unrest we may feel in our minds. We are to desire him for his own sake, not for his gifts but for his gracious being. We are to center our attention on him, letting both wonder and worry fade into forgetting. If distractions interfere with our centering prayer, we are to let them go by and return to a word or phrase that stills our soul.[7] This could be a phrase like "my God" or "I love you" or simply one word like "Jesus" or "mercy." What counts most is our "naked intent" toward God, a movement of

5. *The Ascent of Mount Carmel,* book 2, chapt. 15, in *Collected Works of St. John,* p. 149.

6. *The Cloud of Unknowing,* ed. William Johnston, S.J. (Garden City, N.Y.: Doubleday, Image Books, 1973), pp. 53–55.

7. Ibid., p. 56.

our will to be united with him in the center of our being. We have to learn to be at home in this cloud of unknowing, illumined by a flame of pure faith that asks nothing of God but God himself. We are to return to this bright darkness as often as we can, for herein dwells our entire good who is God, ineffable, merciful, eternally in love with humankind.[8]

In this way one truly approaches contemplation, becoming in the process a living temple of the Spirit of God, a radiant witness to his presence in the world. As a result of this felt intimacy with the Sacred, we are more conscious than ever of sin and of our desire to resist temptation. As we experience absorption in contemplative prayer, so are we more attentive to the voice of conscience. Sin is experienced as a "lump," a uselessly heavy burden pulling us away from our center.[9] We seek friendship with God by fixing our desires on him alone. According to the author of *The Cloud:*

> In itself, prayer is simply a reverent, conscious openness to God full of the desire to grow in goodness and overcome evil. Now we know that all evil, either by instigation or deed, is summed up in the one word "sin." So when we ardently desire to pray for the destruction of evil let us say and think and mean nothing else but this little word "sin." No other words are needed. And when we intend to pray for goodness, let all our thought and desire be contained in the one small word "God." Nothing else and no other words are needed, for God is the epitome of all goodness. He is the source of all good, for it constitutes his very being.[10]

No suffering seems too much to endure to reach such a good. Nothing God asks of us could be refused. We desire only to obey his will. We have experienced for ourselves the truth of

8. See George A. Maloney, S.J., *Bright Darkness: Jesus—The Lover of Mankind* (Denville, N.J.: Dimension Books, 1977).
9. *The Cloud,* p. 94.
10. Ibid., p. 98.

St. John's maxim "Seek in reading and you will find in meditation; knock in prayer and it will be opened to you in contemplation."[11]

At certain moments, we may sense in a manner completely unexpected that the living God has drawn us to himself in an embrace of love that is almost overwhelming. The wound that burned during sensual and spiritual purification is suddenly sweet; the fire that consumed is soothingly benevolent. St. John's writing touches upon this mystery, telling us

> this flame of love is the Spirit of its Bridegroom, which is the Holy Spirit. The soul feels Him within itself not only as a fire that burns and flares within it . . . that flame, every time it flares up, bathes the soul in glory and refreshes it with the quality of divine life.[12]

The darkness of not knowing, which may have been so terrifying at first, is now revealed and befriended as the secret wisdom of God.[13] According to St. John of the Cross, dark contemplation is the mystical theology of which the masters speak, for though it is a secret to the intellect and other faculties, it is a radiant light to the innermost depths of the soul. Unknowing becomes the most profound kind of knowing. Our life is not our own to use and abuse but Christ's holy temple, the dwelling place of his Spirit. This experience propels us to a new depth of commitment to live contemplatively and to serve Christ's kingdom in the world. We move, as we shall see in the next few chapters, from contemplation to compassion, from silent adoration to humble service, from worship to work. We move from the world back to God and from God back into the world.

11. "Maxims on Love" in *Maxims and Counsels,* no. 79, in *Collected Works of St. John,* p. 680.
12. *The Living Flame of Love,* stanza 1, paragraph 3, in Ibid., p. 580.
13. *The Dark Night,* book 2, chap. 17, in Ibid., pp. 368–76.

10

Living Contemplatively

Peace I bequeath to you, my own peace I give you, a peace the world cannot give, this is my gift to you. (Jn. 14:27)

Spiritual masters agree that the gift of Jesus' peace is a true sign of contemplative living. Equanimity, tranquillity, inner radiance, joy—these attitudes characterize one who has received the Lord's peace and now lives as his humble servant in the world. So powerful is this peace that it expands and penetrates our whole physical and psychological life. It is not a peace cheaply won via political or social sloganizing. This peace is the fruit of purification. Its soil is a broken, humbled heart; its harvest is a disciplined, ordered mind.

One cannot be a purveyor of this peace and at the same time castigate either the spiritually or the materially poor. A woman cannot live this peace and feel resentment toward men and vice versa. This peace is both earned and given. The price we pay involves subduing our pride, our arrogant tendency to have all the answers, our refusal to listen to the formative wisdom of the ages. The reward given is awe for the mystery, a refined sense of receptivity to God's will and respect for his people, a willingness to ask the right questions and to live in faith, even if we do not have all the answers. Above all, we grow more responsive to influences that come from God's presence rather than from the pulsations, pressures, and popular slogans that pass for wisdom in the world.

Such peace makes us prefer silence to a series of empty, angry words. It inclines us to seek solitude instead of losing ourselves in faceless crowds or leveling collectivities. If God asks us to suffer the pain of being a sign of contradiction in a world madly in love with the superficial, this peace strengthens us to say "So be it."

Out of this peace comes the thoughtfulness to explore whether or not we *ought* to do something, even if, technically speaking, we *can* do it. The contemplative weighs both the ends of our actions and the means to accomplish them. Uppermost in the mind is concern for the common good, based on respect for each person's unique, Christ-given gifts, not on the will or questionable wisdom of one or a few self-declared prophets.

The contemplative keeps alive the sense of mystery in an era passionately committed to measurement, dehumanization, and depletion of human and natural resources. Thus, for lack of a better phrase, we could call the contemplative "an ecologist of the spirit," a person committed alone or in small groups to the preservation of basic Christian values expressed in the classical sources of our faith and formation tradition and in contemporary sources responsive to that tradition.

The contemplative is aware experientially of the miracle that the whole of one's self, body, mind and spirit, memory, imagination and anticipation, intuition, understanding, and will come from God. One's entire life is an act of total presence to the Transcendent.

St. Catherine of Siena, a true contemplative living in the world, addressed this mystery of union between God and the soul. In one of her prayers, her words rapturously exclaim

> *You,*
> *Godhead,*
> *one in being and three in Persons,*
> *are one vine with three branches—*
> *if I may be permitted to make such a comparison.*
> *You made us in your image and likeness so that,*
> *with our three powers in one soul,*
> *we might image your trinity*
> *and your unity.*
> *And as we image,*
> *so we may find union:*
> *through our memory,*
> *image and be united with the Father,*
> *to whom is attributed power;*
> *through our understanding,*
> *image and be united with the Son,*
> *to whom is attributed wisdom;*
> *through our will,*
> *image and be united with the Holy Spirit,*
> *to whom is attributed mercy,*
> *and who is love*
> *of the Father and the Son.*[1]

By penetrating to the foundations of herself, by stripping away all traces of selfish sensuality, St. Catherine discovered that not she but God is the source of being. She lost the unreal Catherine in order to find the real Catherine in Christ. It was natural for her, already at a young age, to let him take over her whole self and direct her to service of the Church. Her actions

1. *The Prayers of Catherine of Siena,* ed. Suzanne Noffke, O.P. (New York: Paulist Press, 1983), p. 42.

were outflows of God's self-communication, recorded vividly in her *Dialogue*.[2]

The saint wrote frequently about this gift of self-knowledge, granted to her through the grace of infused contemplation. Jesus told her, ". . . Even your own existence comes not from yourself but from me, for I loved you before you came into being."[3] Catherine responded:

> You, Light, have disregarded my darksomeness; You, Life, have not considered that I am death; nor you, Doctor, considered these grave weaknesses of mine. You, eternal Purity, have disregarded my wretched filthiness; you who are infinite have overlooked the fact that I am finite, and you, Wisdom, the fact that I am foolishness.[4]

Christ told her in turn:

> No angel has this dignity, but I have given it to those . . . whom I have chosen to be my ministers. I have sent them like angels, and they ought to be earthly angels in this life.[5]

Catherine accepted this commission to be an "earthly angel" and the demands it would make upon her by asking herself:

> What is her food? God's honor and the salvation of souls. Once she has risen above seeking her own selfish honor she runs like one in love to the table of the cross to seek God's honor. She fills up on disgrace, embracing insults and abuse, conforming herself entirely to the Word's teaching and in truth follows in his footsteps.[6]

2. Catherine of Siena, St., *The Dialogue*, trans. Suzanne Noffke, O.P., in *The Classics of Western Spirituality* (New York: Paulist Press, 1980). Hereafter abbreviated *Dialogue*, followed by chapter and page number.

3. *Dialogue*, chapt. 4, p. 29.

4. *Dialogue*, chapt. 167, p. 364.

5. *Dialogue*, chapt. 113, p. 212.

6. From letter 322 as quoted in footnote 22, *The Prayers of Catherine of Siena*, p. 40.

Contemplatives attain consonance in and through conformity to Christ. Every action they perform is done in dialogue with the Divine Partner. God gives them the gift of his presence, and an immense peace descends upon the soul, consoling and strengthening them, introducing them into his own divine activity. This bonding is only possible to the degree that their self-sufficiency is not only crushed but is also seen to be incompatible with what God wants to accomplish. Docility is not shapeless passivity but a willingness to let God form us increasingly in his image and likeness.

Catherine took the Lord at his word when he said, ". . . I have done and do all I do in providence for your salvation from the beginning . . . right up to the end."[7] Her words summarize the contemplative path in this insightful phrase:

> Souls such as these have let go of themselves, have stripped off their old nature, their selfish sensuality, and clothed themselves in a new nature, the gentle Christ Jesus, my Truth, and they follow him courageously.[8]

Contemplatives experience in a heightened way the Paschal Mystery of dying and rising. God crushes their pride through inner and outer suffering while simultaneously overwhelming them with touches of peace and joy. The soul is left with a terrifying feeling of powerlessness while experiencing a powerful increase of faith, hope, and love. The intensity of God's advances causes torment and intense soul-searching, but this seems a small price to pay in the light of anticipated transformation. It is clear, as in Catherine's case, that contemplation is not a matter of formal education or fantastic imagination out of tune with the repeated truths of a faith tradition. It is the engagement of the entire being in a heart-to-heart relationship with God. It is an eager longing to know Christ crucified and

7. *Dialogue,* chapt. 152, p. 324.
8. *Dialogue,* chapt. 100, p. 189.

to taste the eternal Godhead. When this happens, Christ is to contemplatives as ". . . a peaceful sea with which the soul becomes so united that her spirit knows no movement but in [Christ]. Though she is mortal she tastes the reward of the immortals . . ."[9]

Thus the contemplatives are aware through faith that actions have value only in and through the divine power that animates and guides them. Little by little, God's power is disclosed through our efforts, but no human action, much less our prayers to God, can exist without his prior graces. All comes from and returns to him. God invades the soul by sending it inner lights and deep attractions. A mysterious perception at times accompanies these appeals. We simply see, hear, and understand more of the More Than. This is knowledge derived from faith. The soul suspends its thoughts and movements in order to give all its attention to this compelling Presence. As the psalmist said:

> Yahweh, you examine me and know me,
> . . . behind and close in front you fence me around,
> shielding me with your hand.
>
> (Ps. 139:1, 5)

Because rebellions against God seem increasingly perverse, the contemplatives rely on him to purify any outbursts of pride. Because true independence resides in humility, it is clear that the main obstacle to contemplation is not countless distractions but an egocentric inclination to resist God. This secret determination is rooted in pride, and to temper it is a lifelong endeavor, calling for continual repentance. The saint's sense of sin is not a morbid fixation but an acknowledgement of the reality St. Paul articulated in his letter to the Ephesians:

9. *Dialogue,* chapt. 79, pp. 147–48.

> But God loved us with so much love that he was generous
> with his mercy: when we were dead through our sins, he
> brought us to life with Christ . . . and raised us up with him
> and gave us a place with him in heaven . . . (Ep. 2:4–6)

Though we may continue to falter, stumble, and fall, Christ
is there to help us acknowledge our sinfulness and to repent
from our heart. We feel the tender mercy of God and the call
to alter our motivation to pursue a virtuous life. We move from
fear of punishment to recognition of not loving the One who
loves us so much. Perhaps this is why contemplatives understand so profoundly the mystery the Church refers to as
"happy fault." They see how much good has come out of the
fall of humanity. God continues to give great graces to souls
who are still weak but whom he wishes to bring into the temple of perfect love. St. Paul would be a classic example. His
weakness did not separate him from the Lord but drew him
toward divine wisdom. What saved him was his singleness of
heart, his intention to love God and will the good despite inev-
itable failures. In the purity of his heart, he continued to will
the one thing necessary.[10]

The core of faith remains firm, even if on the periphery we
occasionally falter or feel God's absence more than his presence. Essentially, we belong to God. According to Thomas
Merton, the surest sign of infused contemplation is this:

> . . . Behind the cloud of darkness is a *powerful, mysterious
> and yet simple attraction which holds the soul prisoner in this
> darkness and obscurity.* Although the soul is filled with a sense
> of affliction and defeat, *it has no desire to escape from this arid-
> ity.* Far from being attracted by the legitimate pleasures and
> lights and relaxations of the natural order, it finds them repel-
> lent. All created goods only make it restless. They cannot satisfy
> it. *But at the same time there is a growing conviction that joy and*

10. See Søren Kierkegaard, *Purity of Heart Is to Will One Thing,* trans. Douglas V.
Steere (New York: Harper & Row, Publishers, Inc., Harper Torchbooks, 1956).

*peace and fulfillment are only to be found somewhere in this
lonely night of aridity and faith.*[11]

Far from resting in God in quietistic indifference, contemplation finds its fulfillment in charity. All action springs from this
contemplative center and returns to it. We give ourselves to the
Lord so that he can express himself through us. Hence, Merton concluded:

> There is no contradiction between action and contemplation
> when Christian apostolic activity is raised to the level of pure
> charity. On that level, action and contemplation are fused into
> one entity by the love of God and of our brother in Christ.[12]

Merton and others assure us that contemplation is not a
strange, esoteric phenomenon, accompanied by raptures or ecstatic feelings. It is the work of the Holy Spirit leading our
spirits to compunction, conversion, ceaseless prayer, compassion, and charity. All of us by virtue of our baptism may desire
and pray for this gift of deep, intimate knowledge of God via a
union of love. On our side, it is clear that we must give up our
desires for things that can never fulfill us in order to be at one
with the God in whom is all joy and peace, and from whom we
receive a hundredfold for all we have renounced.

The greatest mistake we can make, spiritually speaking, is to
remain at a distance from God, content to engage in a few
routine exercises of piety and to avoid sin as a matter of moral
duty. We respect God as our maker, but our hearts do not
belong wholly to him. We are still absorbed in our own ambitions, troubles, comforts, anxieties, interests, and fears. When
we do turn to God, it is usually because we want him to sort

11. Thomas Merton, *What Is Contemplation?* (Springfield, Ill.: Templegate Publishers,
    1978), pp. 47–48 (author's italics). I am indebted to this text for several thoughts
    expressed on the following pages.
12. Thomas Merton, *Contemplative Prayer* (New York: Herder and Herder, 1969), p.
    143.

out our difficulties or dispense rewards, but the thought of passionate, committed love embarrasses us.

Such a divided heart cannot become the dwelling place of God; neither can one taste and savor the depths of joy and peace granted to souls who pass over their preoccupations and plunge into the divine abyss, letting God's love enflame and take possession of their minds, intellects, imaginations, and wills. In other words, we must withdraw our desires from the satisfactions and interests the world offers to us as ultimate and listen instead to his reminder that all these things will pass away.

While God may not grant all Christians the grace of infused contemplation, comparable to the state of mystical espousal and marriage described by St. Teresa of Avila, so-called active contemplation is reachable potentially by all.[13] With the help of grace, we can turn our affections to God, obey his commands to the best of our ability, practice the spiritual disciplines, pray ceaselessly, and abandon ourselves to him. We become contemplatives to the extent that we participate in Christ's divine sonship, or, as Thomas Merton says, when our human nature is united in one Person with the infinite truth and splendor of God.[14] At such moments God may lift us into the realm of passive contemplation, if only for a moment.

These experiences strengthen us immensely for our tasks in the world, enabling us to live and work in the company of Christ. As such, the nature of our task does not determine our degree of sanctity. Simple manual laborers, who give themselves to God in their humble tasks, may be as holy in the core of their being as famous mystics. However, no one would deny the inspiring effect, the indelible imprint, these graces make on

13. See *The Collected Works of St. Teresa of Avila*, vol. 2, *The Interior Castle*, trans. Kieran Kavanaugh, O.C.D. and Otilio Rodriguez, O.C.D. (Washington, D.C.: Institute of Carmelite Studies, ICS Publications, 1980).
14. Thomas Merton, *What Is Contemplation?*, p. 30.

our soul. Merton's writing gives the following description of infused contemplation:

> . . . God's greatest gift to the soul. It is a deep and intimate knowledge of God by a union of love—a union in which we learn things about Him that those who have not received such a gift will never discover until they enter heaven.[15]

This gift absolutely transcends the natural capacities of the soul. We cannot acquire it by our own efforts. It is the perfection of charity, an intellectual, intuitive experience of the revelation that God is infinite love, that he has given himself to us as crucified and risen Lord, and that from henceforth our entire life must be a reflection of this love, for it is love alone that matters.

This awareness brings repose to the soul, even though we may still experience dark moments of aridity or an extreme sense of helplessness. Our own pain and turmoil is as nothing compared to this total absorption in the inexplicable love of God, disclosed in solitude and lived out in the world. We are drawn through the night of faith by the power of an intense love we cannot understand. The darkness of this mystery remains, yet our experience renders the mystery brighter than a cloudless day. Life is reduced to one thought, one desire, one conviction: God alone suffices.

Infused love unifies understanding, memory, and will and raises these powers to God. Worldly, perishing things are put in their proper place. We fathom the mystery of a life lived in likeness to the Lord, of what it means to be fully in the world while not being of the world. It may be wise at this stage of our formation journey to validate these experiences in dialogue with a wise and trusted spiritual director. He or she will surely look for concrete evidence that our activity is prompted by union with God rather than by any semblance of personal

15. Ibid., p. 11.

ambition. More than ever, we seek to become a faithful, devout, compassionate, courageous instrument of his love and mercy in the world. Directed by him, we undertake the tasks he has ordained for us. Through our hands, our heads, our hearts, we allow him to communicate to others the depth of his love.

11

Union with God Through Love

Make your home in me, as I make mine in you. (Jn. 15:4)

What does it mean to make our home in God? Rather than answer this question in the abstract, let us ponder the spiritual teachings of a person commissioned by God to serve the Church as a shining example of Christian commitment. Though she lived as a contemplative religious, she would become in many ways a patron saint for people in the world. I am referring to St. Teresa of Avila, who is universally recognized as an outstanding spiritual director, renowned for her unbending faith, and revered as a Doctor of the Church.[1] Wisdom, integrity, intelligence—these qualities and more convince us that she made her home in God. She experienced to the full the trials and errors, joys and rewards of the spiritual life. She struggled to remain faithful in the face of doubt, choosing al-

1. See E. Allison Peers, *Mother of Carmel: A Portrait of St. Teresa of Jesus* (Wilton, Conn.: Morehouse-Barlow Co., 1944).

ways to follow God's will despite the pull of pride. She persevered in her calling, however badly she might have been mis-
understood. Through the uniqueness of her personality, she
radiated the attitudes of Christ.

Whenever St. Teresa wrote or spoke of union with God, one
could feel behind each word the weight of firsthand experience. Her response to questions about the life of the spirit was
always rooted in reality.[2] In her presence, others felt really
understood. She could anticipate their longing for the Lord
and facilitate this quest.

Like all great saints, Teresa enjoyed a personal relationship
with the Lord. The poet Phyllis McGinley captures in a playful poem the nature of their one-to-one encounter. The poem is
entitled "Conversation in Avila."

> *Teresa was God's familiar. She often spoke*
> *To Him informally,*
> *As if together they shared some heavenly joke.*
> *Once watching stormily*
> *Her heart's ambitions wither to odds and ends,*
> *With all to start anew,*
> *She cried, "If this is the way You treat Your friends,*
> *No wonder You have so few!"*
>
> *There is no perfect record standing by*
> *Of God's reply.*[3]

As the poet suggests, God was Teresa's familiar. In fact, she
described prayer as friendly converse with Christ, who loves

---

2. See *The Collected Works of St. Teresa of Avila,* vol. 1, *The Book of Her Life,* trans.
   Kieran Kavanaugh, O.C.D., and Otilio Rodriguez, O.C.D. (Washington, D.C.:
   Institute of Carmelite Studies, ICS Publications, 1976).
3. Phyllis McGinley, "Conversation in Avila," in *A Selection of Contemporary Religious Poetry,* comp. Samuel Hazo (Glen Rock, N.J.: Paulist Press, Deus Books,
   1963), p. 84.

and esteems us as dear friends.[4] We can speak to him informally and ask for what we need or adore him in silent contemplation. What matters is that we remain, as Teresa did, fully human and uncompromisingly faithful to his messages.

Though Teresa was graced with momentary ecstasy, her ordinary lot was agony. She suffered from severe headaches and stomach ailments. She had to defend her life's work before the inquisitors. Her path to God was dangerously disrupted by poor confessors. Yet she persevered in hope. Consolations were occasional, the endurance of crosses continual. What kept her going was meditation on the sacred humanity of Jesus, his suffering, death, and resurrection. She called him Savior, Spouse, Majesty. She experienced him in the center of her soul, in the interior castle, reached only on the road of humility, detachment, and charity. Her life may be seen, therefore, as a song of faith, a cry of hope, an act of love. Her life assures us that intense prayer and dedicated ministry go hand in hand. She was an ideal blend of receptivity and action, of surrender to the will of God and service to his kingdom. She represents the wholesome, balanced Christian life all are called to lead.

Union with God through love means that there ought to be no conflict between spirituality and functionality, between adoration of God and loving attention to those in need, between compassion and competence. At a time when people lament the alienating conditions of modern life, when, as Walker Percy put it, we feel "lost in the cosmos," St. Teresa witnesses to relaxed, joyful, zealous Christian integration.[5]

This integration is at the basis of her famous book, *The Way of Perfection.*[6] In it her words present advice and counsel to

4. See Peter-Thomas Rohrbach, *Conversation with Christ: An Introduction to Mental Prayer* (Chicago: Fides Publishers, 1956).
5. See Walker Percy, *Lost in the Cosmos: The Last Self Help Book* (New York: Farrar, Straus & Giroux, Inc., 1983).
6. *The Way of Perfection,* trans. Kieran Kavanaugh, O.C.D., and Otilio Rodriguez, O.C.D., in *The Collected Works of St. Teresa of Avila,* vol. 2 (Washington, D.C.: Institute of Carmelite Studies, ICS Publications, 1980).

sisters called to live according to the primitive rule of our Lady of Mount Carmel. She wrote it specifically in response to persistent requests from her sisters that she teach them more about prayer.[7] However, experience told her that before she could explain the essence of union with God, it was necessary to depict the atmosphere essential for such a life to flourish. She sensed the wisdom of outlining in detail the steps to the goal they and we are pursuing. She promised to speak in terms of ordinary things all seekers know to be true. She also said that she would confine herself to what she had experienced personally, or seen in others, or received understanding of from the Lord in prayer.[8] Simply put, what dispositions are necessary if one wants to advance in the service of the Lord? In the vast ocean of contemplation, Teresa will launch us on three safe ships—three trustworthy carriers of human and Christian formation.

> Do not think, my friends and daughters, that I shall burden you with many things; please God, we shall do what our holy fathers established and observed, for by walking this path they themselves established they merited this title we give them. It would be wrong to seek another way or try to learn about this path from anyone else. I shall enlarge on only three things, which are from our own constitutions, for it is very important that we understand how much the practice of these three things helps us to possess inwardly and outwardly the peace our Lord recommended so highly to us. The first of these is love for one another; the second is detachment from all created things; the third is true humility, which, even though I speak of it last, is the main practice and embraces the others.[9]

Her teaching here is basically the same as that found in the Gospel. The mark of transformation in Christ, of union with

7. Ibid., p. 39.
8. Ibid., p. 40.
9. Ibid., p. 54.

God through love, presupposes obedience to his commands, but this means much more than external adherence to rules and regulations. Transformation of heart is an inner experience of accepting ourselves in humility as God's gift. Letting go of powers, pleasures, and possessions that place our ego at the center of life calls for detachment. Loving one another in a generous, self-donating way leads to charity, the hallmark of Christian life.

This threefold path of formation, when sincerely practiced, will lead to peace. If we put into practice these basic dispositions, we will live in the light of Christ's peace and by implication enjoy the rest and refreshment of the Holy Spirit in contemplative prayer. These three directives, pertaining to humility, detachment, and charity, address not only Carmelite sisters but all who are seeking a life of personal intimacy with God. Teresa's insights are not confined to a specific locale in sixteenth-century Spain. *The Way of Perfection* spans the ages and is rightly designated a classic. The examples Teresa used to embellish each of these dispositions necessarily contain some time-bound accretions, but her underlying intuition about the centrality of these directives is timeless.

The truest humility implies listening to who we most deeply are. It is less a focus on our misery and more an awareness of God's mercy. He became one of us so that we might become more like him, fully human and fully in tune with the symphony of God's providential plan for our lives.

Detachment or poverty of spirit consists in being ready to respond to what the Lord desires us to do. It is not a question of negating the good things of life but of redirecting them away from our control toward God's glory.

Charity or chaste, respectful love is the most challenging directive Christ gives us, for it means leaving behind such obstacles as jealousy, conceit, competitiveness, and discourtesy and fostering such conditions as confirmation, discretion, empathy, and respect. Such worldly honors as fame, status, popularity, and acclaim become secondary to living the hidden life of prayer and good works.

Maturation in the life of the spirit depends partly on the love we receive from parents, friends, and peers. Love received increases our capacity to give love in return. The formation of humanity in compassion depends on this uniquely human capacity to love one another beyond the self-preserving instinct.

We lose our freedom by clinging excessively to other people or by grasping possessions in an inordinate way. We lose our peace when people disappoint us or we fail them. Wealth, fame, and worldly accomplishments pale in importance as the years pass. Even if we do not focus consciously on detachment, it happens to us. We are detached from our parents and our careers by the liberating agents of aging, illness, retirement, and death. Teresa felt obliged to teach that detachment from passing people, events, and things is essential so that we can be liberated for the Eternal.

To love unselfishly, to let go of obstacles to freedom, to follow God's call, we must learn day by day the painful truth of who we are. The basic fact of being human means being made by God in his image and likeness. We are not sufficient unto ourselves. We depend for our life itself on the formation mystery, on the God who calls us forth from *humus,* from the dust of the earth. We have been made in his image, in accordance with the Christ-form in the core of our being. This constitutes our original dignity, our substantial union with God, a union that can never be destroyed. The fall into pride and sin separated us from God. We were exiles in a land of unlikeness. Human pride marred our likeness to God, but through the mediation of Jesus, Lord and Savior, we gained the help we needed to reenter the land of likeness.

Humility embraces the two foundations of charity and detachment, for it reminds us at once that God loved us first and that we are called to sever the bonds that keep us from returning to him in the union of love. Humility signifies the misery that evoked God's mercy, the nothingness that he raises to the heights of nobility.

These three directives apply not only to human formation; they also impart in a lively way the wisdom of the Christian revelation. To love one another is ultimately only possible because God has first loved us (1 Jn. 4:10). To live realistically in detachment leads us from the bondage of pride to the freedom of the children of God, who lay aside their former way of life and acquire a fresh, spiritual way of thinking (Ep. 4:22–3). To be humble is to imitate Christ, who humbled himself for our sakes, becoming one of us in all things but sin (Ph. 2:6–7).

We experience intimacy with others by uniting ourselves with the Lord, who alone can teach us the art of selfless loving. We detach ourselves from narcissistic needs so we can cultivate true community with Christ at the center. We gain our deepest spiritual identity when we give up our egocentric striving for perfection.

Thus Christian spirituality as such is built on the three pillars of charity, renunciation, and truth, or of love for one another (chastity), detachment (poverty of spirit), and humility (obedience). Chaste, respectful loving, letting go of excess, listening to God's will as disclosed in each situation—these three foundations guide the spiritual life of Christians in the world as much as they provide the basis for a vowed religious commitment.

Teresa's treatment of this trinity of virtues reveals the realistic, humorous, gentle quality of her gifts as a director of formation. Eloquent and shrewd, observant and penetrating, she disclosed the essential framework of a life in Christ that simultaneously respects uniqueness and fosters community. The way she proposed is simply a portrait of her own person. She was not only writing about love, detachment, and humility.

She was herself a living witness to their validity as foundational directives of human and Christian formation.

In regard to the first directive—love for one another—Teresa was well aware that we err either because our love is excessive or defective. We love too much or too little, too possessively or too indifferently. The problem of possessive love is especially treacherous in the close confinement of a contemplative community, where it may flourish under the guise of virtue and piety. However, such love, directed toward anyone but God, becomes a detriment to the soul that ought to be primarily occupied with loving him. In keeping with her own experiences, Teresa cautioned that this excessive love is likely to be found in a house where no more than thirteen women live. Its symptoms, well known to her, are outlined in the following text:

> . . . failing to love equally, all the others; feeling sorry about any affront to the friend; desiring possessions so as to give her gifts; looking for time to speak with her, and often so as to tell her that you hold her dear and other trifling things rather than about your love for God. For these great friendships are seldom directed toward helping one love God more. On the contrary, I think the devil gets them started so as to promote factions in religious orders. For when love is in the service of His majesty, the will does not proceed with passion but proceeds by seeking help to conquer other passions.[10]

Again, while Teresa was addressing the sisters, she could have been addressing people in a college department, where factions are often the rule more than the exception. She could have been talking to girls in a dormitory, employees in a company, parish councils, members of a large family. Instead of cultivating in a domineering way one friend over another, Teresa said

10. Ibid., p. 55.

that all must be friends, all must be loved, held dear, helped. The Lord does not play favorites and neither must we.

To clarify further this basic principle of community life, Teresa's words distinguish between two kinds of love: purely spiritual or unselfish, and spiritual mixed with sensuality or selfishness. The first love takes into account our affective, somewhat controlling nature, but does not stop there. Compared to the greater love of God that grips every fiber of one's being, lesser loves for pleasure and power seem like shadows. Other loves weary one compared to the endless refreshment of the love of God. One does what one can and must do for others, but one avoids becoming preoccupied with their lives to the point of becoming forgetful of God.

Perfect lovers detach themselves from the comforts the world has to offer since they cannot tolerate being apart from God. No affliction is too great for such a love, no sacrifice too much to ask. Such lovers are more inclined to give than to receive, for theirs is a ". . . precious love that imitates the Commander-in-chief of love, Jesus, our Good!"[11] This love is happiest when it sees others progressing likewise in nonmanipulative, nonseductive, self-donating service.

These latter traits—manipulation, seduction, self-serving versus self-giving—characterize the lesser love Teresa's words caution us to avoid at all costs. If we keep Christ as our model, we will feel compassion and respond accordingly to each person's needs. We will cultivate truly spiritual friendships, take time for recreation, and keep the commandments with great perfection. Phrases like "my life," "my soul," "my only good," will be words of endearment, kept only for our Lord.

Teresa was adamant about the elevation of love from sensual to spiritual union. Firmness must guide gentleness in this regard. She said, for example, that if any nun is found to be the

11. Ibid., p. 65.

cause of such disruption, it is best to send her to another monastery.[12] Trouble follows trouble when people focus exclusively on one another and refuse to acknowledge their mutual dependence on the Lord.

In regard to the second directive—detachment from all created things—Teresa's words immediately cast this rather negative-sounding disposition in a positive light. She said that detachment ". . . if it is practiced with perfection, includes everything . . . because if we embrace the Creator and care not at all for the whole of creation, His Majesty will infuse the virtues."[13] Teresa was in no way advocating a posture of hatred or disparagement of creation. She was obviously a religious poet, a lover of life and nature. What her writing does advise is an inner attitude of carefreeness from the vicissitudes of creation. All things come and go, rise and fall, stay for a while and pass away. If we become absorbed in these things, we lose our freedom. We can no longer soar without worry to God.

The solution is not to despise creation but to embrace the Creator. In this way we come to see all persons, events, and things in their proper order and relationship. What is ultimate is God alone. All else has to be seen as but a pointer to the One in whom and by whom everything exists in the first place. Withdrawal from everything is thus a condition for the possibility of being united entirely with God and through him gaining everything anew. Lacking this inner stance of respectful distance or poverty of spirit, we become victims of worldly ambitions and impulses. Letting go of external possessions is not enough; one must let go of any excessive interior attachments, no matter how pious they seem.

In this regard, Teresa tackled a concrete problem she may have had trouble with herself: attachment to relatives other than one's parents, for they ". . . seldom fail to help their

12. Ibid., p. 71.
13. Ibid., p. 71.

children, and it is right for us to console them in their need."[14]
As contemplatives must discipline their relations to friends,
loving all equally, so they must moderate their memories, anticipations, and fantasies where relatives are concerned. The
mortification implied here is mainly an interior reformation of
past, future, and current images and concerns. If one vows to
transform self and world in the image of God, one must be
ready to respond to the Lord's directive to leave mother, father, brothers, and sisters to follow him (Mk. 10:28–30).

Teresa did not like us to fool ourselves. We leave the world
in its worldliness and go into the desert, where the real work of
detachment begins: disentangling ourselves from bodily comforts that lead to disobedience; avoiding heroic penances that
lack discretion and increase vanity; practicing silence; ceasing
to complain about slight sicknesses, since "when the sickness
is serious, it does the complaining itself"; in short, we begin to
practice the "long martyrdom" of interior mortification.[15]
Only if we go against our own will, gradually without knowing
how, relying on grace, shall we find ourselves at the summit.
St. Teresa would agree with St. John of the Cross that the way
is rigorous, but the reward is great, for in giving up all, we gain
the All.

Teresa insisted that humility goes hand in hand with charity
or love of others and with detachment or diminished seeking
of self-satisfaction. It is the ground of these dispositions and
the source of our strength, especially when it comes to resisting demonic plays on human pride. Great progress in holiness occurs when we resist vain reasonings and defensive pos-
tures; take on lowly tasks; avoid the privileges of rank and
power; disengage ourselves from excesses of praise or blame;
and bear with dishonor, ridicule, and misunderstanding, for

---

14. Ibid., p. 74.
15. Ibid., pp. 79, 82.

". . . it calls for great humility to be silent at seeing oneself condemned without fault."[16] She added:

> The truly humble person must in fact desire to be held in little esteem, persecuted, and condemned without fault even in serious matters. If she desires to imitate the Lord, in what better way can she do so?[17]

Only in this way do we model our lives on the humility of Jesus and Mary with real determination, not wavering for reasons of worldly honor.

In one of her most memorable comparisons, Teresa's words place humility within a game of chess. She said:

> The queen is the piece that can carry on the best battle in this game, and all the other pieces help. There's no queen like humility for making the King surrender. Humility drew the King from heaven to the womb of the Virgin, and with it, by one hair we will draw Him to our souls. And realize that the one who has more humility will be the one who possesses Him more; and the one who has less will possess Him less. For I cannot understand how there could be humility without love or love without humility; nor are these two virtues possible without detachment from all creatures.[18]

In this beautiful text, Teresa summed up her program of formation in the virtues of charity, detachment, and humility. This formation is both a preparation for and a consequence of the practice of silence, spiritual reading, meditation, and prayer. She did say emphatically that ". . . meditation is the basis for acquiring all the virtues, and to undertake it is a matter of life and death for all Christians."[19] By the same token, to progress to the higher stage of contemplation or union with God through love, one must put these three virtues into

16. Ibid., p. 91.
17. Ibid., p. 91.
18. Ibid., p. 94.
19. Ibid., p. 94.

constant practice, for they must be possessed in as high a degree as possible as a prerequisite for contemplative prayer. "I say that the King of glory will not come to our soul—I mean to be united with it—if we do not make the effort to gain the great virtues."[20]

Contemplatives must diligently practice self-denial lest their state of life breed a proud, holier-than-thou attitude. They ought to seek the lowly path so God himself can lead them higher. For ultimately contemplation is his gift, not our doing. Teresa herself was unable for many years to practice meditation without reading a book. Lack of delights in contemplation enabled her to walk with humility, in great security, waiting upon the Lord's will. She affirmed in this regard that ". . . true humility consists very much in great readiness to be content with whatever the Lord may want to do . . . and in always finding oneself unworthy to be called His servant."[21]

Enduring trials is truly good for the soul. Contemplatives can wager they are on the right path if they ". . . keep the flag of humility raised and suffer all blows they receive without returning any."[22] Bearing the cross without complaint signifies growth in Christlike love. Such love is another sign that we are on the way to union. For real advancement is manifested in deeds done for our own spiritual growth and for the good of others, ". . . not in having more delights and raptures in prayer, or visions, or favors of this kind that the Lord grants . . ."[23] There is more wisdom in detaching ourselves from these extraordinary phenomena than in pursuing them under the guise of spiritual awakening. Here humility joins mortification and careful obedience of the rules governing the common life.

In conclusion, Teresa said:

20. Ibid., p. 95.
21. Ibid., p. 101.
22. Ibid., p. 104.
23. Ibid., p. 104.

. . . these are the virtues I desire you to have . . . the ones
you must strive for and about which you should have only holy
envy. As for those other devotions, there's no need to be sorry
about not having them; having them is an uncertain matter. It
could be that in other persons they may be from God, whereas
in your case His Majesty may permit them to be an illusion of
the devil and that you be deceived by him, as were other persons
. . . Why desire to serve the Lord in a doubtful way when you
have so much that is safe?[24]

Anyone, in any walk of life, seeking liberation from egoism
and union with the Lord in this world, can benefit from her
advice and counsel. Her words offer sensible, clear directives
to all. Humility assures us that we shall find our most unique,
congenial self in Christ. Detachment enables us to live in each
situation with a high degree of compatibility. We can be simultaneously near to others in genuine care while maintaining a
certain respectful distance. Charity flows over into compassion
for our own weaknesses and for the vulnerability of those who
people our world. If we love Christ as the center of our life, we
can serve the Church tirelessly while maintaining inner tranquillity.

St. Teresa's life remains thus a living witness to the marriage
of ministry and mysticism. This marriage is grounded in
humility, detachment, and love. These dispositions constitute a
trinity of virtues modeled on the Triune Mystery and embod-
ied fully in Jesus Christ. He is the humble, detached, charita-
ble Person we are called to be like, whether we go forth in
service or seek solitude and silence.

On the contemporary scene, we find the same basics of spirituality lived beautifully by Mother Teresa of Calcutta. She too
is a person of profound wisdom and down-to-earth works.
Nothing is more attractive than a person who remains as fully
human as she, while being utterly capable of managing a great

24. Ibid., p. 105.

work for the Church. Whether ours is a labor of headline quality or household simplicity, the same principles are true. We must live the foundations of Christian spirituality in the public as well as in the private sphere. It is for this reason that we who seek union with God through love turn for final inspiration and guidance to the Mother of Christ.

The events of Mary's life are well known to us, but have we ever explored the essentials of spiritual deepening to which they are pointing? Have we ever related these events to our everyday experience and to our quest for a fully human, fully Christian spirituality? Let us journey with her on this pilgrimage of faith, hope, and love. The stages that unfold in her life will inevitably touch our own as we seek ever deeper union with God in this world in anticipation of our lasting union with him in the life to come.

Mary, prior to the annunciation, probably lived a rather ordinary life of devotion. She trusted God and desired to obey his will as conveyed through scripture to the chosen people. Then she heard the angel's voice. How unexpected, how unforeseen was this event. It shattered her expectations and filled her with fear. Like any conversion experience, it left her deeply disturbed. She felt as we would if God turned our plans upside down and thrust us into unknown realms of risk and darkness. Conversion is an essential element of the spiritual life. It always entails a rupture of complacency, a break with the past, a turning around, a fresh start. It beckons us to make a leap of faith into a new form of life by saying yes to God, even if we do not see all the implications of our response. Mary moved from girlhood to womanhood at this moment. She became wholly receptive to God's will, faithful to his divine plan in the highest possible degree.

Following conversion, we may experience, as Mary did, a time of joyful exaltation. Anything seems possible. We want to share the good news with anyone who will listen. We see this urgency to share jubilation in Mary's visit to Elizabeth. She greeted her cousin with a lofty outburst of gratitude and joy, declaring herself to be the handmaiden of the Lord. She knew that God is her strength, that he will transform her poverty into a powerful witness to his potency. This enthusiasm prevails throughout the nativity experience. Christ, born through Mary, is born anew in each of us. Conversion or breakthrough to a new level of spirituality is thus followed closely by heartfelt joy and accompanying consolations. Alas, the journey in faith is far from over, as we learn again from Mary's experience.

Events like the flight into Egypt, the presentation of Jesus in the Temple, accompanied by Simeon's warning that a sword would pierce her heart, the losing and finding of Jesus in the Temple—all signaled a new stage of spiritual deepening for her: that of desolation, sorrow, and crushed expectations. Enthusiasm gives way to sober reminders of life's limits. The reins of control slip out of our hands as God's mysterious plan takes over. His ways are beyond what our feeble minds can grasp. All we can do is live in faith. A higher meaning will be revealed if we can wait upon God's word in a spirit of patient endurance and gradual detachment from our own dreams of the way things should be. Though our expectations break down in this desertlike experience, it leads us to a breakthrough to still deeper ranges of spirituality. But the worst is not over yet. Detachment is one thing, death is another.

When Mary watched her son leave their home in Nazareth to begin his public life, she, like all mothers, knew she would have to let go of little things like caring for his health, seeing that he had enough to eat, giving him a warm place to sleep. But what words could be found to describe her sorrow in witnessing his death. Something in her died with him. She knew the stark pain of powerlessness, of being able to do nothing except stand in numb helplessness with the other women at the foot of the cross. She died completely to herself, as we must do, in order to live completely in and for God. Unless the seed go underground and be buried, it cannot bring forth new buds. At this supreme moment of poverty, humanly speaking, God gave Mary and each of us a mission. In her nothingness, she entered fully into the divine plan of salvation.

Thus we enter the stage of transformation, empty of self that we may be full of God. Dying with Christ, we become a channel through which God's saving love can be mediated to humankind. We collaborate with the work of salvation, conscious of our call to make the Paschal Mystery a lived reality in our personal life and in the lives of all those entrusted to our care.

These stages—conversion, consolation, desolation, death, and transformation—are essential components of the Christian life, as illustrated so vividly in Mary's faith journey. The sooner we learn to surrender our self-centeredness, the more open we shall be to the fullness of peace and joy only Christ can give. Married or single, actively involved or quietly secluded, we become who we are meant to be by becoming the receptive, strong, serene, and capable persons God has called us to be from the beginning.

12

Serving God in the World

I tell you most solemnly, whoever believes in me will perform the same works I do myself, he will perform even greater works, because I am going to the Father. (Jn. 14:12)

The fruits of silence, reading, meditation, prayer, and contemplation are at work in the entire Church. These spiritual exercises form an essential part of our ministry as people in the world. We want to deepen our inner resources so that we can become more faithful instruments of God in our families and professions. We know that holiness is not a private possession granted to select souls but a universal call issued to each of us. It is not to be equated with ecstatic feelings or extraordinary phenomena. Holiness is loving God with our whole being and radiating that love in every dimension of life and world.

Flowing from contemplation and all that readies us for this gift is the life of dedicated, Christlike service. If service is insufficiently rooted in contemplative presence, it may lead to arrogance and activism out of touch with our original intention. We work to attain our own success with little consideration for what God may be asking of us.

Our projects need to be rooted in contemplation. In stillness, we can listen to God's directives and do our best to execute them gently but firmly in the given situation. Whether we succeed or fail is not the point. What counts for God is our willingness to try. Contemplation enables us to be serenely present in the world, doing what we can, without succumbing to the ways of the world. We remain rooted in the love of God while going forth in labors for the kingdom.

This rhythm of recollection and participation is an essential feature of Christian commitment. Whatever we happen to be doing—cooking a meal, writing a letter, teaching a class, nursing the sick—we do out of love for God and a desire to make this love manifest. We want to help others see his face in every person, event, and thing. This is what it means as Christians to be missioned. Missionary duty is not limited to evangelizing work in foreign lands. It is what we are to do every day in our homes and professions. Whether we are involved in teaching, law, nursing, medicine, or social work, whatever our position or profession, we have to remain faithful disciples despite daily pressures.

Someone stops me in the hall just to chat when I have a mile-high stack of work to finish on my desk. I want to be warmly attentive to her, but the work I have to do pulls me away. Later, when I recall what occurred, I feel guilty because of my curt behavior. Why couldn't I have been more courteous to her? Is it because I have allowed my prayer life to slip into the background under the illusion that work as such is prayer? I know if I succumb to the pressure to perform efficiently, I'll risk losing compassion.

I tried to express these same thoughts in a letter to a friend, who, like myself, feels caught up in daily pressures to the exclusion of quiet, inner presence.

I enjoyed so much reading your letter and learning firsthand of your retreat experience. It sounds as if you utilized the occasion for recentering yourself around the Lord and for drawing strength from him so that you can be a consoling, formative presence for all who cross your path.

Certainly a key theme that emerged for you was the necessity to make room in your life for the refreshing experience of silence and solitude. Slowing down and dwelling are important directives not only for spiritual reading but for life as a whole. When we are too pressured, too rushed, too concentrated on our task, too eager to keep things under control and make everything work perfectly, we lose ourselves, we lose our peace, we lose our center. By contrast, it is only when we work from that still and silent center, integrated around the Lord, that we can produce well and respond fully to the people he wants us to touch. It helps a great deal if we can maintain our sense of humor, including the ability to laugh at ourselves and not to take things too seriously.

While you were on retreat, you regained, as we all must, a truly transcendent perspective. Let us continue to remind each other how necessary it is not to lose the long-range view of eternity, becoming so caught up in time that we forget what ultimately matters, which is our life of intimacy with God.

Our society teaches us to fear failure, always to try harder. A competitive spirit, a clever tongue, an analytical mind— these qualities may place one in the so-called winner's circle, but they overlook the need for personal appreciation and confirmation. Love of success may destroy the duty to love our neighbor.

A good nurse, for instance, is conscious that her patients not only need physical care but a kind word as well. Sick as they may be, encounter in a human sense is always appreciated, even if it is communicated only by a touch on the forehead or hand. We respond badly to mere functional treatment. We wince at whatever reduces us to numbers or forms to be processed in as short a time as possible. The nurse who takes time to listen to her patients responds instinctively to these humane aspirations. What matters most is not her schedule or her coffee break, but the people entrusted to her care. Her energies and talents must be placed first of all at their service.

Christian service attends to and cares for others in one's here and now situation. There is no split between who we are and what we do. We display outwardly the spiritual values we keep alive inwardly. Others sense in this caring presence an integration between what goes on in our hearts and what happens in the consulting office, hospital, law firm, union meeting, or whatever. It is not unusual to hear people say, "Your heart is really in your work, isn't it?"

Christian service is thus not an altruistic ideal but a real commitment to be helpful and inspiring through our relaxed yet skillful care. That is why others may remember, "It was not so much what you said or did so well but the way you were. That meant more to me than words can contain, and I'll always be grateful."

Maintaining this quality of care involves a lifelong effort. In the deepest sense, it is sustained by all that we experience and learn in and through silence, spiritual reading, meditation, prayer, and contemplation. These practices assure us that we do not have to carry the world on our shoulders; we do not need to develop a savior complex; we do not have to keep our lives under rigid, perfectionistic control. We can trust that God is with us, that he embraces all who are in need.

This attitude of hope enables us to continue to be of service to others despite discouragement, failure, and disappointment. Though we may not always be able to see the light at the end of the tunnel, we believe that something ultimately good will come out of our service and that in time we will understand its meaning more fully.

If we neglect our spiritual exercises or grow lax in faith,

hope, and love, we run the risk of becoming depleted when the first blush of enthusiasm about our service gives way to the sober reality of routine. It is possible in that case that the burnout syndrome begins to manifest itself.[1] Initial enthusiasm is good, for it symbolizes our intention to make the world a better place, to help people become happier. What causes trouble is the exalted nature of our intentions insofar as these tend not to be rooted in realistic appraisal of the situation and of our own limits and talents.[2] Our pride stands in the way of our seeing clearly what can and cannot be done. "I" want to cure the ills of the world; "I" want to resolve the blatant causes of social injustice; "I" want people to shake themselves out of this torpor of complacency and act decisively *now!*

After a while this initial enthusiasm wears off. We detect the vast difference between our exalted aspirations for what should be and the reality of what is or what can be done on the basis of our limited capacity. In short, we discover that things are not working out as we had hoped they would. We struggle to retain our dreams, though we witness them being dashed against the harsh buttress of reality. We sense intuitively that something is wrong without knowing exactly why. Our intentions were so good, but we are simply not there the way we used to be. It is harder and harder to get started.

We may begin to feel negative toward people and unhappy about ourselves. We wonder what we are really doing to help them. No one seems to pay attention to our ideas. We may continue to look and act the part of the devoted professional, playing well the role of the teacher, the physician, the social

1. See Jerry Edelwich, *Burn-Out: Stages of Disillusionment in the Helping Professions* (New York: Human Sciences Press, 1980).
2. For a comprehensive consideration of appraisal in relation to the formative or deformative consequences of social presence, see Adrian van Kaam, "Provisional Glossary of the Terminology of the Science of Foundational Formation," *Studies in Formative Spirituality* 3, no. 1 (February 1982): 123–54.

worker, but our heart is not in it. We have to force ourselves to keep up appearances.

According to Adrian van Kaam, we may respond to such a state in either a negative or a positive way.[3] In the former case, we become more or less indifferent. "They don't care about me, so why should I care about them? I'll do my job, draw my pay, and for the rest—let them take care of themselves." We do exactly what we have to do in order not to be fired, but no more. We opt to maintain the proper codes of behavior, mastering well the rubrics appropriate to our profession, but the price we have to pay for this negative solution is high. A dreadful strain develops between our life as such and our work. There is a growing split between who we are and what we do.

A more positive solution to the crisis involves a renewal of our commitment to Christ and the willingness to suffer whatever is necessary for his sake. Perhaps we need to find a quiet place for reflection or seek a few days of retreat to regain this faith perspective. It may be necessary to create a little space between ourselves and the immediate work situation to see what is happening to us and to foster a more positive solution. It is never too late to catch the process of depletion of dedication in time and to begin to reverse it.

It helps considerably if we can give up our illusions of perfectionism as well as our idle expectations that life will proceed according to our plans and projects. To be of service is to remain open to surprises, while developing a flow-with-what-comes-and-make-the-best-of-it attitude. Such a realistic approach enables us to cope with the crisis of commitment itself. We can admit what we appreciate and what we resent, what we agree to live with and what we can seek to improve. Rather than letting bad feelings fester, we try to find creative

3. Van Kaam's analysis of a negative or positive solution to the social presence crisis can be found in Ibid.: 125–26.

solutions that bring peace to our heart and make peace in a formerly tense situation. Though this crisis may repeat itself, each time it does we can deal with it as a positive challenge, leading to a more lasting sense of dedication. In other words, we seek to disclose Christ's call hidden beneath the superficial upsets found in every professional situation.

It is also necessary to open ourselves again and again to the gifts of faith, hope, and love.[4] To believe in the ultimate goodness of life, to hope that things will be better tomorrow than they are today, to love those entrusted to our care—these basic dispositions correct the problems of discouragement, depletion of dedication, and closure to compassion. We can be gentle and kind because we recognize how vulnerable all of us are. We have to try to live in peace despite the tension that will always be present between the right to be who we are and the real limits of every human situation.

If we are at peace within ourselves, not demanding perfection, then we can be peacemakers for others. Christ asks us as his disciples to live peacefully, justly, mercifully, even if others display opposite tendencies. We can never underestimate the power of being a *living witness* to what we believe. In this regard, actions do speak louder than words. People remember who we are, even if they do not recall exactly what we said. What impresses them is our peaceful, just, and compassionate presence.

I once knew a housepainter who had remarkable musical talent. He played an excellent jazz guitar, but he also had eight mouths to feed. He remained a painter and practiced during weekend jam sessions. He knew in his heart that what he wanted to do most of all was to accept an offer with a local group or traveling band. Still his family's well-being came first.

4. According to van Kaam, formative social presence is nourished by one's abandonment in faith, hope, and consonance, or love, to the beneficial meaningfulness of the mystery of formation. See Ibid.: 123.

His decision to stay in the building business was made out of his sense of justice and mercy. Hence, he was able to experience peace and joy in that profession.

Our style of presence may have to change if our way of communicating to people is rigid, bossy, withholding, suspicious, irritable, quick, uninspired. Our opinions may be inflexible instead of open to moderation. We fail to take into account the uniqueness of each person. We may always expect others to bend to our way, insisting on the last word. We demand that others change, not us. We may be afraid to widen our circle of friends for fear of not being the center of attention.

In this light, it may be helpful if we move out of familiar settings to fresh encounters with challenging, stimulating people. Our encounters, besides being recreative, serve to restore friendly relations. People do not perceive us as self-sufficient professionals, seeking autonomous power, but as persons dedicated to caring for one another in all kinds of circumstances. We are able, so to speak, to co-vibrate with others, to co-experience, at least imaginatively, what they are going through. Such a disposition is essential in a profession like nursing or teaching. It also helps parents to relate to their children. It means, in effect, that we accept others as they are, that we reverence their uniqueness, that we bless them and wish them well.

To be empathetic is to feel what the other is feeling in a heart-to-heart moment. Such an appreciative stance invites others to put their best foot forward. They want to show us that our trust in them is not unfounded. They know that we may have to make practical judgments, but they also know that we appreciate their ultimate worthwhileness and unique potential.

This disposition also enables us to appreciate the discouragement people around us are feeling. We see depression everywhere: in college dormitories, in families, among teenagers, in successful professionals. We can appreciate this plight and help people appraise it wisely because we have been there ourselves. Even though we may not have gone through their actual experience of depletion, we can imagine what it is like. Empathy enables us to help others get through a crisis; it also makes us more inclined to be compassionate toward ourselves when we discover that we are drifting into a similar predicament.

According to van Kaam, we need to be mindful of the need others feel for empathic communication.[5] In our times we have developed a wealth of sophisticated techniques telling us how to talk to one another. Yet people still complain of not being listened to or understood.[6] We seem to say too little or too much. Hospital patients frequently lament that their health care specialists are too busy to really listen. They praise the quality of care they are receiving in one breath while bewailing poor communication in the next. Verbal communication is important at such times, especially when taking the patient's history, but so too is the art of nonverbal communication via a gesture, a smile, a touch of hands.

All of us have this capacity for empathic communication, but in many it remains underdeveloped. What seems to be missing is the joy that is only possible to maintain if we have abandoned ourselves to the mystery of Christ present in every person. How else can we explain the sense of jubilant peace that radiates from the face of a Mother Teresa of Calcutta as she walks among the destitute and the dying? Neither injustice, suffering, nor death can shake the confidence of her smile. Such transcendent joy is spontaneous and contagious. It cannot be forced. It wells up from deep within the soul. It is present even when we must weep, for it is rooted in faith, hope, and love.

5. See Ibid.: 142.
6. Mortimer Adler reflects on this predicament in his acclaimed book, *How to Speak, How to Listen* (New York: Macmillan Publishing Co., Inc., 1983).

In conclusion, we can say that the joyous person is like a light on the mountain. He or she moves like a dancer in tune with the rhythms of life, its peaks and valleys. Gracious, open, receptive, gentle, joyful—with these dispositions he or she responds to the Lord's injunction to do the works he does and ones even greater than these (Jn. 14:12). Some are called to serve in soup kitchens, others in research laboratories; it all depends on who we are. What matters is that we remain gently alert and quietly open to any invitation to service that the Lord issues.

We may only advance forward inch by inch, but it is better than falling back. No matter how weak we feel, we can always turn to the abiding strength of the Lord, who comes to us most regally when weakness is at its worst. Then we hear him saying, "My grace is enough for you; my power is at its best in weakness" (2 Co. 12:9–10). Like St. Paul, we can willingly boast of our limits so that the life of Christ may grow within us.

> So I shall be very happy to make my weaknesses my special boast so that the power of Christ may stay over me, and that is why I am quite content with my weaknesses, and with insults, hardships, persecutions, and the agonies I go through for Christ's sake. For it is when I am weak that I am strong. (2 Co. 12:10)

If Christianity is a religion of the word, read carefully and reflected upon, it is also an invitation to work hard for the betterment of the world. We must go into the desert with Jesus, knowing all the while that the test of our relationship will come when we walk with him on the dusty road. Our meeting with him in silence is but the beginning of a lifelong response to being missioned. As he tells us at the end of the Gospel of St. Mark, "Go out to the whole world; proclaim the Good News to all creation" (Mk. 16:16).

Epilogue

We can serve the restoration of spirituality in our era by returning to the foundations that have formed the basis of this book, namely, silence, formative reading, meditation, prayer, contemplation, and service. By living these foundations we avoid two dangers: pietism and functionalism. The Christian spiritual life is neither a matter of trans-worldly ascetical practices, leading to self-satisfying piety, nor of social activism, leading to functional, this-worldly reform while neglecting spiritual sustenance. If the first exaggeration breeds a spiritualism lived from the neck up, the second swings from elation over projects to be accomplished to depletion when these crash against the rugged shores of reality.

Reality is helplessness. Reality is aging, suffering, dying. It is vulnerability and lack of control. It is what we refuse to see because it is so near. Christ calls us to face reality and go through it to the vision he grants of redemption, rebirth, peace, and joy. All else passes, but this vision perdures. The service we render others is best fulfilled when we help them to keep the vision of hope from disappearing entirely.

If the truth were known, many live on the borderline of despair. Look at their eyes behind makeup and polite masks. So many seem distant, vacant, sad. They are the lambs who have lost their way. To them Christ sends his servants to rekindle dying hope, to call what is dead to live again. Helplessness then becomes a sacrament of hope. Deprivation becomes an avenue to liberation when we realize we do not stand alone. As servants of the mystery, we can assure others on the basis of our own experience that Christ is with us, now and always.

These foundations of spiritual formation take into account the whole person. They attend to our transcendent longing as well as to our functional responsibility to proclaim the Gospel to all nations. In the words of Thomas Merton, all of us are called to be "contemplatives in a world of action." The harmony that is our goal involves a lifelong effort, but what encourages this pursuit is the promise of integration on all levels of our person. We are to be Christ's servants in the world without becoming slaves of the world.

We know when we are in the presence of a true servant of the Lord, for in him or her we see the cross of suffering and the empty tomb of resurrection. We behold in flesh and blood the Paschal Mystery. Such is the picture I hold in my mind of an old priest I must leave unnamed. He had been imprisoned by anti-Christian forces for many years behind the Iron Curtain. His career as a missionary was a total failure by convert-making standards. He had been into the caverns of doubt and despair, but through the grace of God he had clung to the thread of faith. Abandonment to holy providence, together with endless repetitions of the Lord's Prayer, were his salvation. Now he spends his days praying, writing, greeting people who come to him, as they came to the desert fathers of old, seeking a word of solace for their troubled souls.

One can see in the grooves etched on his face that he has gone through torture. His skin is a map of suffering, yet it is nearly transparent with light. He anticipates what a person wants to ask while listening with compassion to each story. He says that nothing matters in the end, nothing but God. If we are with God, all will be well. If we depart from him, no happiness is possible.

These are simple words, stark words. Yet they pierce the heart. In the mirror of his transcendent smile, one sees that it is true—nothing matters but God. In the servant's presence, the questions one came with dim to silence. One waits without asking why. The servant's touch is light and respectful. For some reason one feels thoroughly understood and accepted. This man is a living witness of God's love, a mirror of his tender mercy. As he is, so may we be.

BIBLIOGRAPHY

Adler, Mortimer. *How to Speak, How to Listen.* New York: Macmillan Publishing Co., Inc., 1983.

Augustine, St. *The Confessions of St. Augustine.* Translated by John K. Ryan. Garden City, N.Y.: Doubleday & Co., Inc., Image Books, 1960.

Benson, Herbert. *The Relaxation Response.* New York: William Morrow & Co., Inc., 1975.

Bloom, Anthony. *Living Prayer.* Springfield, Ill.: Templegate Publishers, 1966.

Carretto, Carlo. *Letters from the Desert.* Translated by Rose Mary Hancock. Maryknoll, N.Y.: Orbis Books, 1972.

Carrington, Patricia. *Freedom in Meditation.* Garden City, N.Y.: Anchor Books, Doubleday & Co., Inc. 1978.

Catherine of Siena, St. *The Dialogue.* Translated by Suzanne Noffke, O.P. *The Classics of Western Spirituality.* New York: Paulist Press, 1980.

Cummings, Charles. *The Mystery of the Ordinary.* San Francisco: Harper & Row Publishers, Inc., 1982.

da Todi, Jacopone. *The Lauds.* Translated by Serge and Elizabeth Hughes. *The Classics of Western Spirituality.* New York: Paulist Press, 1982.

Dauenhauer, Bernard. *Silence: The Phenomenon and Its Ontological Significance.* Bloomington, Ind.: Indiana Univ. Press, 1980.

de Caussade, Jean-Pierre. *Abandonment to Divine Providence.* Translated by John Beevers. Garden City, N.Y.: Doubleday & Co., Inc., Image Books, 1975.

de Foucauld, Charles. *Meditations of a Hermit.* Translated by Charlotte Balfour. New York: Orbis Books, 1981.

Dillard, Annie. *Pilgrim at Tinker Creek.* New York: Bantam Books, Inc., 1975.

Edelwich, Jerry. *Burn-Out: Stages of Disillusionment in the Helping Professions.* New York: Human Sciences Press, Inc., 1980.

Eiseley, Loren. *The Unexpected Universe.* Middlesex, England: Penguin Books, Inc., 1973.

Flannery, Austin, O.P., general ed. *Vatican Council II: The Conciliar and Post Conciliar Documents.* Collegeville, Minn.: Liturgical Press, 1975.

Franck, Frederick. *The Zen of Seeing: Seeing/Drawing as Meditation.* New York: Random House, Inc., Vintage Trade Books, 1973.

Frank, Anne. *The Diary of a Young Girl.* Translated by B. M. Mooyaart-Doubleday. New York: Modern Library, Inc., 1952.

Hall, Edward. *The Dance of Life: The Other Dimension of Time.* Garden City, N.Y.: Doubleday & Co., Inc., Anchor Books, 1983.

Hammarskjöld, Dag. *Markings.* Translated by Leif Sjoberg and W. H. Auden. London: Faber & Faber, Inc., 1964.

Hauser, Richard J. "Keeping a Spiritual Journal: Personal Reflections." *Review for Religious,* July–August 1983, pp. 575–84.

Hazo, Samuel, comp. *A Selection of Contemporary Religious Poetry.* Glen Rock, N.J.: Paulist Press, Deus Books, 1963.

John of the Cross, St. *The Collected Works of St. John of the Cross.* Translated by Kieran Kavanaugh, O.C.D., and Otilio Rodriguez, O.C.D. Washington, D.C.: Institute of Carmelite Studies, ICS Publications, 1973.

John XXIII, Pope. *Journal of a Soul.* Translated by Dorothy White. New York: McGraw-Hill Book Co., 1965.

Johnston, William, S.J., *Christian Zen.* New York: Harper & Row Publishers, Inc., 1971.

———, Editor. *The Cloud of Unknowing.* Garden City, N.Y.: Doubleday, Image Books, 1973.

Juliana of Norwich, *Showings.* Translated by Edmund Colledge, O.S.A. and James Walsh, S.J. New York: Paulist Press, *The Classics of Western Spirituality,* 1978.

Kierkegaard, Søren. *Purity of Heart Is to Will One Thing.* Translated by Douglas V. Steere. New York: Harper & Row Publishers, Inc., Torchbooks, 1956.

Leclercq, Jean, O.S.B. *The Love of Learning and the Desire for God: A Study of Monastic Culture.* Translated by Catherine Misrahi. New York: Fordham Univ. Press, 1961.

Levinson, Daniel J. *The Seasons of a Man's Life.* New York: Alfred A. Knopf, Inc., 1978.

Lindbergh, Anne Morrow. *Gift from the Sea.* New York: Random House, Inc., Vintage Trade Books, 1965.

———. *Bring Me a Unicorn.* New York: Harcourt Brace Jovanovich, Inc., 1971.

Maloney, George A., S.J. *Bright Darkness: Jesus—The Lover of Mankind.* Denville, N.J.: Dimension Books, 1977.

Merton, Thomas. *What Is Contemplation?* Springfield, Ill.: Templegate Publishers, 1978.

———. *Contemplative Prayer.* New York: Herder and Herder, 1969.

———. *Thoughts in Solitude.* Garden City, N.Y.: Doubleday, Image Books, 1968.

Merton, Thomas, trans. *The Wisdom of the Desert: Sayings from the Desert Fathers of the Fourth Century.* London: Sheldon Press, 1974.

Muto, Susan Annette. *Celebrating the Single Life: A Spirituality for Single Persons in Today's World.* Garden City, N.Y.: Doubleday & Co., Inc., 1982.

————. *Blessings That Make Us Be: A Formative Approach to Living the Beatitudes.* New York: Crossroad Publishing Co., 1982.

————. *Renewed at Each Awakening: The Formative Power of Sacred Words.* Denville, N.J.: Dimension Books, 1979.

————. *The Journey Homeward: On the Road of Spiritual Reading.* Denville, N.J.: Dimension Books, 1977.

————. *A Practical Guide to Spiritual Reading.* Denville, N.J.: Dimension Books, 1976.

————. *Steps Along the Way: The Path of Spiritual Reading.* Denville, N.J.: Dimension Books, 1975.

————. *Approaching the Sacred: An Introduction to Spiritual Reading.* Denville, N.J.: Dimension Books, 1973.

Newman, John Cardinal. *Apologia pro Vita Sua.* Garden City, N.Y.: Doubleday & Co., Inc., Image Books, 1956.

Noffke, Suzanne, O.P., ed. *The Prayers of Catherine of Siena.* New York: Paulist Press, 1983.

Peers, E. Allison. *Mother of Carmel: A Portrait of St. Teresa of Jesus.* Wilton, Conn.: Morehouse-Barlow Co., 1944.

Percy, Walker. *Lost in the Cosmos: The Last Self Help Book.* New York: Farrar, Straus & Giroux, Inc., 1983.

Picard, Max. *The World of Silence.* Translated by Stanley Godman. South Bend, Ind.: Gateway Editions, 1952.

Raguin, Yves. *Paths to Contemplation.* Religious Experience Series, vol. 6. St. Meinrad, Ind.: Abbey Press, 1974.

Rohrback, Peter-Thomas. *Conversation with Christ: An Introduction to Mental Prayer.* Chicago: Fides Publishers, 1956.

Squire, Aelred. *Asking the Fathers: The Art of Meditation and Prayer.* New York: Paulist Press, 1973.

Teresa of Avila, St. *The Book of Her Life.* The Collected Works of St. Teresa of Avila, vol. 1. Translated by Kieran Kavanaugh, O.C.D., and Otilio Rodriguez, O.C.D. Washington, D.C.: Institute of Carmelite Studies, ICS Publications, 1976.

————. *The Way of Perfection* and *The Interior Castle.* The Collected Works of St. Teresa of Avila, vol. 2. Translated by Kieran Kavanaugh, O.C.D., and Otilio Rodriguez, O.C.D. Washington, D.C.: Institute of Carmelite Studies, ICS Publications, 1980.

Therese of Lisieux, St. *Story of a Soul: The Autobiography of St. Therese of Lisieux.* Translated by John Clarke, O.C.D. Washington, D.C.: Institute of Carmelite Studies, ICS Publications, 1975.

Thomas à Kempis. *The Imitation of Christ.* Edited by Harold C. Gardiner. Garden City, N.Y.: Doubleday & Co., Inc., Image Books, 1955.

Thoreau, Henry David. *Walden.* Edited by Sherman Paul. Boston: Houghton Mifflin Co., Riverside Editions, 1957.

van Kaam, Adrian. *Formative Spirituality.* Fundamental Formation, vol. 1. New York: Crossroad Publishing Co., 1983.

———. "Provisional Glossary of the Terminology of the Science of Foundational Formation." *Studies in Formative Spirituality 3* (February 1982): 123–54.

———. *The Transcendent Self: The Formative Spirituality of Middle, Early and Later Years of Life.* Denville, N.J.: Dimension Books, 1979.

———. *Woman at the Well.* Denville, N.J.: Dimension Books, 1976.

———. *In Search of Spiritual Identity.* Denville, N.J.: Dimension Books, 1975.

———. *Spirituality and the Gentle Life.* Denville, N.J.: Dimension Books, 1974.

———, and Susan Annette Muto. *Practicing the Prayer of Presence.* Denville, N.J.: Dimension Books, 1980.

Wells, Ronald V. *Spiritual Disciplines for Everyday Living.* Schenectady, N.Y.: Character Research Press, 1982.

Zimmerman, Michael. "Heidegger and Heraclitus on Spiritual Practice." *Philosophy Today* 27 (Summer 1983): 87–103.

About the Author

DR. SUSAN ANNETTE MUTO is Director of the Institute of Formative Spirituality and Managing Editor of its two journals, *Studies in Formative Spirituality* and *ENVOY*. A native of Pittsburgh, she completed her undergraduate degree at Duquesne University and her graduate studies in literature at the University of Pittsburgh.

After a brief career in journalism and public relations, she became Assistant Director of the Institute in 1965, a position that changed the direction of her life and led her into her present dedication to teaching, speaking, writing, and research in the field of foundational human and Christian formation.

As a single laywoman, living her vocation in the world and supported by over eighteen years of experience in the Institute, Dr. Muto is more than qualified to address the spiritual concerns of laity, clergy and religious. In addition to her administrative and academic responsibilities as a professor in the Institute's master's and doctoral programs, Dr. Muto is a prolific author and a renowned speaker, both nationally and internationally.

Dr. Muto is the eldest of three children. Her mother lives in the Pittsburgh vicinity, as do her two brothers and their families. She enjoys traveling, theater productions, films, art shows, and the symphony. Her time is also spent in doing what she loves most—reading and writing within the framework of the Christian formation tradition, especially as it is recorded in the writings of both pre- and post-Reformation spiritual masters.

This book is a complement to her previously published *Celebrating the Single Life*. Both books aim to respond to the present hunger for spiritual deepening expressed by people in the world.